Contents

Name _____

 1.

 **Rr**

2.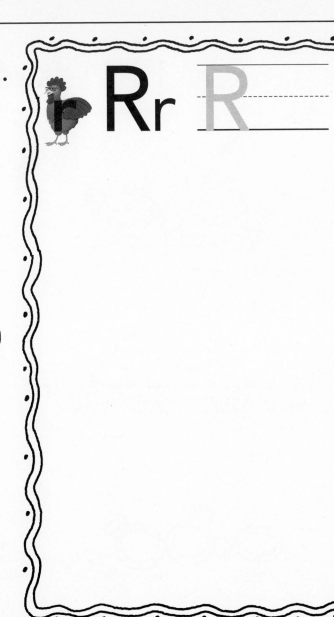

Rr **R** _____ **r** _____

Children
- draw lines from pictures whose names start with the sound for *r* to *Rr*
- write *Rr* and draw something else for that sound in the box with Reggie Rooster

 Home Connection
Let me tell you which picture names start with the sound for *r*. Then let's look for things at home whose names start with the sound for *r*.

71

Name _____

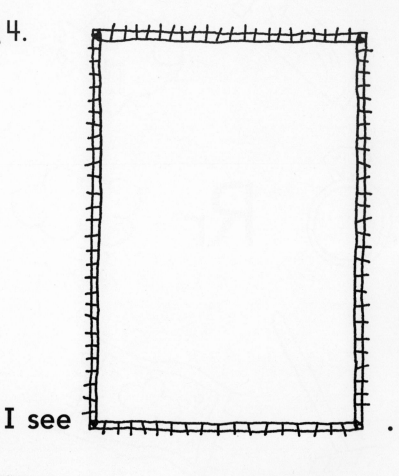

I   see

 1.

_____

- - - - - - - - - - -

I _____ .

2.

_____

- - - - - - - - - - -

_____ see .

3.

_____

- - - - - - - - - - -

I _____ .

 4.

I see _____ .

THEME 2: Colors All Around
Week Three
High-Frequency Word Review *I, see*

Children
for 1, 2, and 3,
- read the sentence and write *I* or *see* to complete it

for 4,
- read the sentence and draw a picture to complete it

Home Connection
I am learning to read the words *I* and *see*. Let me read this cartoon to you and tell you what I see.

Name _____

1.

2.

THEME 3: We're a Family
Week One *Jonathan and His Mommy*
Characters/Setting

Children
1. draw the family member the boy in the story took a walk with
2. color pictures of things the story characters saw when they jumped, skipped, and danced through their neighborhood together

 Home Connection
Let me tell you about a story called *Jonathan and His Mommy* and what they saw when they took a walk.

73

Name _____

1.

2.

THEME 3: We're a Family
Week One *Jonathan and His Mommy*
Responding

Children

1. draw themselves on a neighborhood walk with one of their family members

2. draw what they might see on their walk

 Home Connection
Let me tell you about the pictures I drew. On our next walk, let's see what we see that Jonathan and his mommy saw.

Name _____

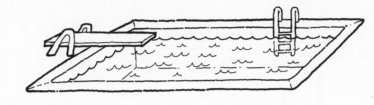

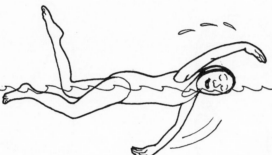

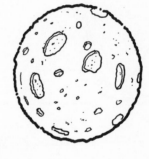

THEME 3: We're a Family
Week One _Tortillas and Lullabies_
Characters/Setting, Responding

Children
- circle the pictures that show characters a story might be about
- color the pictures that show places a story might tell about
- draw a line between each character and a place it might be

Home Connection
Let's think of some other characters who could be in stories and draw places they might be.

Name _____

T t   T   t

THEME 3: We're a Family
Week One
Phonics: Initial Consonant *t*

Children
- write *Tt* at the top
- name the pictures Tiggy Tiger thinks about
- color and write *t* beside pictures whose names begin with the sound for *t*

Home Connection
Next time we watch TV together, let's look for things whose names start with the sound for *t*.

Name _____

I see my

1.

I _____ my  .

2.

_____ see my  .

3.

I see _____  .

4.

I see my 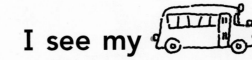 .

THEME 3: We're a Family
Week One
High-Frequency Words Review *I, see, my*

Children
- for 1, 2, and 3, read the sentences and write *I*, *see*, and *my* to complete them
- for 4, draw a picture to go with the sentence

Home Connection
Let me read these sentences to you. Then let's think of other spotted things a clown might tell about.

81

Just for fun, color the pictures of families. How many people are in each picture?

Name _____

THEME 3: We're a Family
Week Two *Goldilocks and the Three Bears*
Drawing Conclusions

Children
- color the pictures that give clues about which of the Three Bears will be the most unhappy when the bears get home
- draw a picture of that bear

Home Connection
Let me tell you about this picture. Which bear do you think will be most upset to see what Goldilocks has done?

83

1.

2.

3.

4.

THEME 3: We're a Family
Week Two *Goldilocks and the Three Bears*
Responding

Children
- for 1, 2, and 3, color the picture that shows the way they might have told the bears they were sorry if they had been Goldilocks
- for 4, draw another way Goldilocks might have apologized

 Home Connection
Let me tell you about these pictures and how I think Goldilocks should have told the bears she was sorry.

Name _____

THEME 3: We're a Family
Week Two
Phonemic Awareness: /b/

Children
- color all the pictures on pages 85 and 86 that start like *Benny Bear*
- cut and paste the pictures for that sound in the boxes on page 86
- draw something else that starts with that sound

 Home Connection
Let's name all the things on the front and back that start like *Benny Bear*.

85

Name _____

Name _____

1.

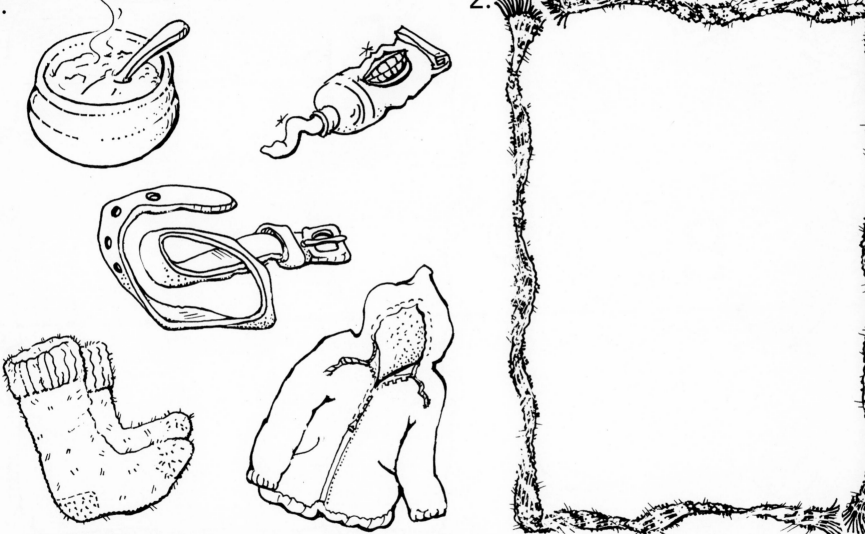

2.

THEME 3: We're a Family
Week Two *Shoes from Grandpa*
Drawing Conclusions, Responding

Children
1. color what else Jessie's family members might get her if she gets the jeans she asked for at the end of the story
2. draw some kind of clothing they might wish for as a birthday gift

Home Connection
Let me tell you a story called *Shoes from Grandpa*. Then let's talk about who the members of our family are.

Name _____

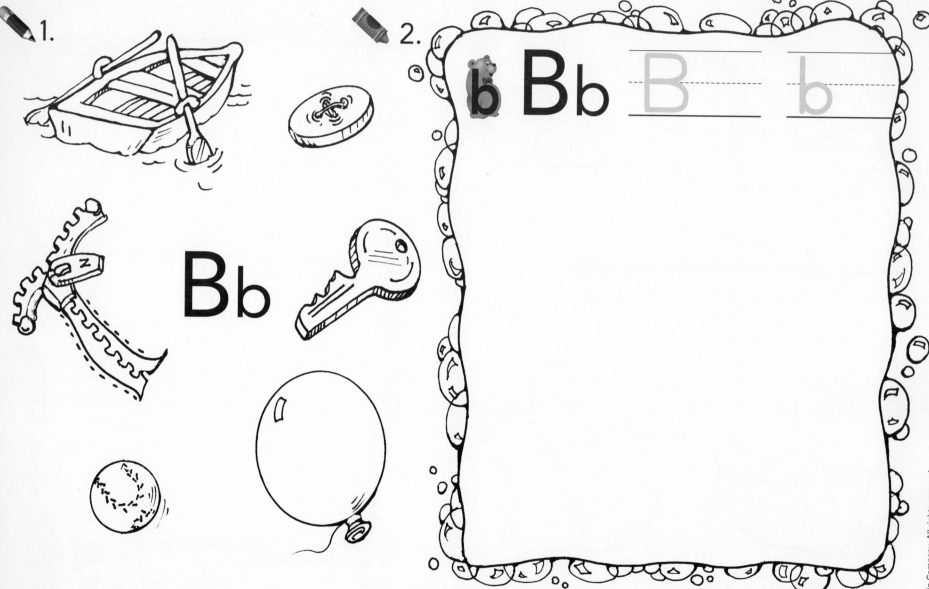

1.

2.

b B b   B   b

Bb

THEME 3: We're a Family
Week Two
Phonics: Initial Consonant _b_

Children
• draw lines from pictures whose names start with the sound for _b_ to _Bb_
• draw something else for that sound in the box with Benny Bear

Home Connection
Let me tell you about the picture I drew. Then let's look for more things whose names start with the sound for _b_.

Name _____

THEME 3: We're a Family
Week Three
Phonemic Awareness: /n/

Children
- color all the pictures on pages 95 and 96 that start like *Nyle Noodle*
- cut and paste pictures for that sound in the boxes on page 96
- draw something else that starts with that sound

Home Connection
Let's name all the things on the front and back that start like *Nyle Noodle*.

95

Name _____

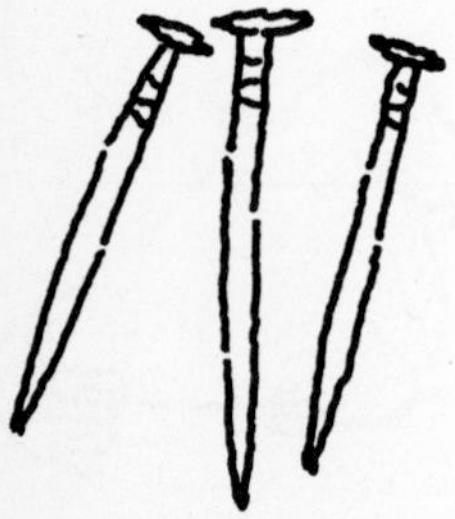

THEME 3: We're a Family
Week Three
Phonemic Awareness: /n/

Name _____

1.

2.

THEME 3: We're a Family
Week Three _Tortillas and Lullabies_
Character/Setting, Responding

Children

1. think about something one of the people in the story did in the kitchen and draw a picture of her doing that

2. think about something one of the people in the story did in the garden and draw a picture of her doing that

 Home Connection
Let me tell you the story we heard today called _Tortillas and Lullabies_. Then maybe we can look at pictures of my grandmothers and great-grandmothers.

97

Name _____

N n   N   n

THEME 3: We're a Family
Week Three
Phonics: Initial Consonant _n_

Children
- write _Nn_ at the top
- name the pictures Nyle Noodle thinks about
- color and write _n_ beside pictures whose names begin with the sound for _n_

Home Connection
Let's look in a newspaper for pictures of things that start like _Nyle Noodle._

Name _____

like   my

1. **I like my**  .

2. **I like** _____  .

3. **I** _____ **my** .

4. **I like** _____  .

THEME 3: We're a Family
Week Three
High-Frequency Words Review *my, like*

Children
• read the sentences and write *like* and *my* to complete them

 Home Connection
Let's write *like* and *my* on a piece of paper. Then I can make up sentences with these words and you can write my sentences.

99

Name _____

1. n **Nn** N n  _____

_____

2. 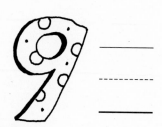 _____

 _____

 _____

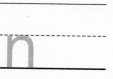 _____

 _____

 _____

3.

THEME 3: We're a Family
Week Three
Phonics: Initial Consonant *n*

100

Children
- for 1 and 2, write *Nn* beside the pictures whose names start like *Nyle Noodle*
- for 3, draw two things that start with the sound for *n*

Home Connection
Let me tell you about the things on the page that begin with the sound for *n*.

Name _____

1.

2.

n N n   N   n

THEME 3: We're a Family
Week Three
Phonics: Initial Consonant *n*

Children

1. draw lines from pictures whose names start with the sound for *n* to N*n*

2. write N*n* and draw something else for that sound in the box with Nyle Noodle

 Home Connection
Let me tell you about the picture I drew. Then let's look for more things whose names start with the sound for *n*.

Name _____

I   my   like   See

1.

See _____  .

2.

_____ my  .

3.

_____ like my  .

4.

I _____ my  .

THEME 3: We're a Family
Week Three
High-Frequency Words Review *my, like, I, see*

Children
• read the sentences and write *I*, *my*, *like* and *See* to complete them
• draw a picture to go with sentences 2 and 4

 Home Connection
Let me read the sentences to you. Then we can cut apart the words at the top and use them with cut-out magazine words to make other sentences.

Name _____

1.

2.

3.

THEME 4: Friends Together
Week One _Friends at School_
Organization and Summarizing

Children
1. think about the friends in the story and color the pictures
2. draw something one group of friends did together in the story
3. color those things the friends played with in the story

 Home Connection
Today my teacher read us a story _Friends at School_. Let me tell it to you. I'll use the pictures to help me remember parts of it.

103

Name _____

THEME 4: Friends Together
Week One *Friends at School*
Responding

Children
- draw what they and a friend might do with each of the school-related things

 Home Connection
Ask me what kinds of things I like to do with my friends. What did you like to do with your friends at school when you were my age?

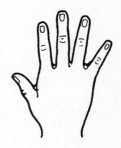

THEME 4: Friends Together
Week One
Phonemic Awareness: /h/

Children

• color all the pictures on pages 105 and 106 that start like *Hattie Horse*

• cut and paste pictures for that sound in the boxes on page 106

• draw something else that starts with that sound

Home Connection
Let's name all the things on the front and the back that start like *Hattie Horse.*

105

Name _____

THEME 4: Friends Together
Week One
Phonemic Awareness: /h/

Name _____

 1.  **Hh** H H h h

2.

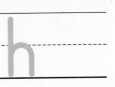 _ _ _ _ _ _ _ _ _

_____

 _ _ _ _ _ _ _ _ _

_____

 _ _ _ _ _ _ _ _ _

_____

 _ _ _ _ _ _ _ _ _

_____

 _ _ _ _ _ _ _ _ _

_____

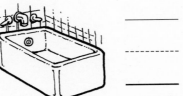 _ _ _ _ _ _ _ _ _

_____

3.

THEME 4: Friends Together
Week One
Phonics: Initial Consonant *h*

Children
- for 1 and 2, write *h* beside the pictures whose names start like *Hattie Horse*
- for 3, draw a picture of two things whose names start with *h*

 Home Connection
Today we learned the letter *h*.
Help me find pictures in books of things that start like *Hattie Horse*.

107

Name _____

a

1.

See _____ ⭐ .

🙂 ☹️

2.

See _____ ☁️ .

🙂 ☹️

3.

See _____ 🐰 .

🙂 ☹️

4.

See _____

THEME 4: Friends Together
Week One
High-Frequency Word: *a*

Children
For 1, 2, and 3
• read the sentences and write *a* to complete them
• mark yes (smile) or no (frown) to show whether the pictures go with the sentences
For 4, read the sentence and draw something they would like to see

Home Connection
Let me read these questions to you and we can see if you answer them the same way I did.

Name _____

A B C D E

F G H I J K

L M N O P

Q R S T U

V W X Y Z

My name is

_____

- - - - - - - - - - - - - - - - - - - -

_____

THEME 4: Friends Together
Week One *Aaron and Gayla's Alphabet Book*
Text Organization & Summarizing, Responding

Children
- name the letters of the alphabet
- color the letter that begins their own name
- write their name on the line
- draw a picture of themselves

Home Connection
Will you sing the ABC song with me? We can point to the letters as we sing.

Name _____

| h | b | c |

  a t

I see a _____ .

   a t

I see a _____ .

  a t

I see a _____ .

 THEME 4: Friends Together
Week One
Phonics: *h, -at*

Children
- write letters to complete the picture names
  (*bat, hat, cat*)
- write each word to complete the sentences

 Home Connection
Let's cut out the letter squares,
mix them up, and build the
words *hat, bat,* and *cat* again.

Name _____

s → at _____

h → at _____

b → at _____

I see a cat _____ .

A fat rat _____ .

I see Nat at _____ .

Children
• add letters to build *hat*, *sat*, and *bat*
• write each word to complete the sentences

Home Connection
Would you like to listen to me
read the words and sentences on
this page? Then we can make up
some other -at words.

111

Name _____

a see like

1.

_____

_ _ _ _ _ _ _ _

I see _____ cat I like.

2.
_____

_ _ _ _ _ _ _ _

I see a hat I_____.

3.
_____

_ _ _ _ _ _ _ _

I _____ a bat I like.

4.

I see a

THEME 4: Friends Together
Week One
High-Frequency Words Review: _a, see, like_

Children
- for 1, 2, and 3 write _a_, _see_, or _like_ to complete the sentences
- for 4, draw a picture to complete the sentence

Home Connection
Let me read these cartoons to you. Then we can cut them into four smaller pages and make a comic book and a cover for it.

Name _____

1.

2.

THEME 4: Friends Together
Week Two *The Lion and the Mouse*
Cause and Effect

Children
1. color what made the mouse afraid
2. color the picture that shows what its promise to the lion caused the mouse to do

Home Connection
Let me tell you the story *The Lion and the Mouse*. Then you'll know what caused the mouse to chew a hole in the net.

113

Name _____

1.

2.

THEME 4: Friends Together
Week Two _The Lion and the Mouse_
Responding

Children

1. imagine they were the author of the story and draw a picture to show a different way the mouse might help the lion

2. draw a picture of a friend in need of help and how they might help that friend

 Home Connection
Today we heard a story called _The Lion and the Mouse_. Will you listen as I tell it to you? Then I'll tell you about the pictures I drew.

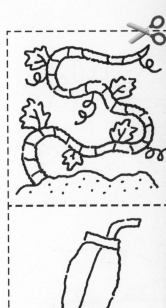

THEME 4: Friends Together
Week Two
Phonemic Awareness: /v/

Children
- color all the pictures on pages 115 and 116 that start like *Vinny Volcano*
- cut and paste pictures for that sound in the boxes on page 116
- draw something else that starts with that sound

Home Connection
I'll name the pictures on the front and back that start like *Vinny Volcano*. Then let's find things around the house that start with that sound.

115

Name _____

THEME 4: Friends Together
Week Two
Phonemic Awareness: /v/

Name _____

1.

2.

V v

V v

THEME 4: Friends Together
Week Two
Phonics: Initial Consonant v

Children

1. draw lines from pictures whose names begin with the sound for *v* to the letters *Vv*

2. write *Vv* at the top and complete the picture of the exploding volcano

 Home Connection
Today I finished this exploding volcano picture. Let me show it to you. Then I can tell you about the other pictures that begin with the sound for *v*.

Name _____

cat

to _____

bat

I like _____ see my cat.

I like _____ see a bat.

THEME 4: Friends Together
Week Two
High-Frequency Word: *to*

Children
• read the words that name the pictures and write *to*
• read the sentences and write *to* to complete them
• draw pictures to go with the sentences

Home Connection
I can read these sentences to you. Then I'll tell you about the pictures I drew to go with the sentences.

Name _____

THEME 4: Friends Together
Week Three *Stone Soup*
Cause and Effect

Children
- think about the story *Stone Soup* and how the man tricked the villagers into making wonderful soup
- color those ingredients that caused the soup to become so tasty and add two more things that could be added to make it even better

 Home Connection
We heard the story *Stone Soup* today. Ask me to tell you about it. I can point to the pictures I colored as I tell that part of the story.

123

Name _____

THEME 4: Friends Together
Week Three *Stone Soup*
Responding

124

Children
- think about whether the stone had anything to do with making the soup tasty
- imagine how the story would be different if the man asked for help making some stone pizza instead
- draw their ideas

Home Connection
Let me tell you about my picture and the story I drew it for.

Name _____

THEME 4: Friends Together
Week Three
Phonemic Awareness: /c/

Children
- color all the pictures on pages 125 and 126 that start like *Callie Cat*
- cut and paste pictures for that sound in the boxes on page 126
- draw something else that starts with that sound

 Home Connection
Let's name all the things on the front and back that start like *Callie Cat*.

Name _____

MILK

THEME 4: Friends Together
Week Three
126   Phonemic Awareness: /c/

Name _____

A B C D E F _ _ _
H I J K L M N
O P Q R S T
U V W X Y Z

_ _ _
A B _ D E F G
H I J K L M N
O P Q R S T
U V W X Y Z

A B C D E
F G H I J K
L M N O P
Q R S T U
V W X Y Z

THEME 4: Friends Together
Week Three *Aaron and Gayla's*
Alphabet Book
Text Organization and Summarizing,
Responding

Children
• write the letters missing from the alphabet
• play this game in pairs: one partner covers a
  letter with a coin or token, and the other tells
  what letter is covered

 Home Connection
Today I learned to play "Hide
the Letter." I can teach it to you.

127

Name _____

Cc   C   c

THEME 4: Friends Together
Week Three
Phonics: Initial Consonant c

Children
- write *C c* at the top
- name the pictures *Callie Cat* thinks about
- color and write *c* beside pictures whose names begin with the sound for *c*

Home Connection
Today we learned the letter *c*. Can you help me find a few things around our house that start like *Callie Cat*?

Name _____

a to see

1. _____

  _ _ _ _ _ _ _ _ _ _ _ _ _ _

I sat _____ see a 🐕 .

2. _____

  _ _ _ _ _ _ _ _ _ _ _ _ _ _

I sat to _____ a 🦆 .

3. _____

  _ _ _ _ _ _ _ _ _ _ _ _ _ _

I sat to see _____ 🐍 .

4. I sat to see a cat.

Children
- for 1, 2, and 3, read the cartoons, write _a_, _to_, and _see_ to complete the sentences, and color the cartoons
- for 4, draw a cartoon to go with the sentence

Home Connection
Listen while I read these cartoons to you. Then we can cut them apart to make a comic book.

Name _____

| cat   mat   fat   sat |

_____

See my fat _____ .

_____

I see a _____ .

My _____ cat _____ .

 THEME 4: Friends Together
Week Three
Phonics: *c, -at*

Children
- write words ending in *-at* to complete the sentences
- mark smile (yes) or frown (no) to show whether the picture goes with the sentence

Home Connection
Let's write *cat, mat, fat,* and *sat* and make up some more sentences using these words.

130

Name _____

h   s   N

☐ **a   t**

I see _____ at bat.

☐ **a   t**

My rat _____ .

☐ **a   t**

I like my _____ .

THEME 4: Friends Together
Week Three
Phonics: *-at* **Words**

Children
• write *h*, *s*, or *N* to complete the words (*Nat*, *sat*, *hat*)
• write each word to complete the sentences about the pictures

Home Connection
Can I read these sentences to you? Then we can cut out the letter squares, mix them up, and use them to build the words *Nat*, *sat*, and *hat* again.

Name _____

to   My   like   a

1.

_____
- - - - - - - - - - - -
_____ cat sat.

_____
- - - - - - - - - - - -
I _____ my cat.

2.

_____
- - - - - - - - - - - -
See _____ rat?

3.

_____
- - - - - - - - - - - -
My cat ran _____ see a
rat.

4.

Children
- for 1, 2, and 3, read the sentences and write words to complete them
- for 4, draw a picture to show how the story might end

Home Connection
I can read these sentences to you. Then I'll tell you about the picture I made that shows how the story ends.

Name _____

1.

2.

THEME 5: Let's Count!
Week One: *Benny's Pennies*
Categorize & Classify

Children
1. draw presents Benny bought for his family
2. draw presents Benny bought for his family's pets

Home Connection
Ask me to tell you about a story
called *Benny's Pennies*.

Name _____

1.

2.

THEME 5: Let's Count!
Week One *Benny's Pennies*
Responding

Children

1. draw things they would buy members of their own families and the pennies it might take to buy each

2. draw things they would buy for a friend and the pennies it might take to buy each

 Home Connection
Can you help me think of some good gifts for our family?

134

Name _____

THEME 5: Let's Count!
Week One
Phonemic Awareness: /p/

Children
- color all the pictures on pages 135–136 that start like *Pippa Pig*
- cut and paste pictures for that sound in the boxes on page 136, then draw something else that starts with that sound

Home Connection
Let's name all the things on the front and the back that start like *Pippa Pig*.

135

Name _____

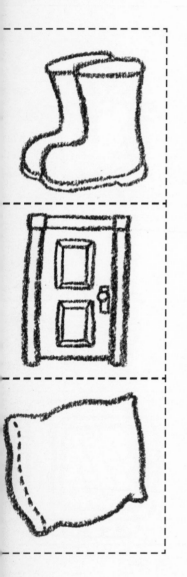

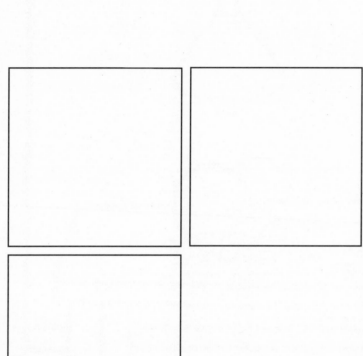

Name _____

1.  P Pp P ____ ____ p ____  ____ ____ ____

2.

3.

THEME 5: Let's Count!
Week One
Phonics: Initial Consonant _p_

Children
- for 1 and 2, color and write _p_ beside the pictures whose names start like _Pippa Pig_
- for 3, draw pictures of two _p_ things

 Home Connection
Today we learned the letter _p_.
Help me find pictures of things
that start with the sound for _p_.

Name _____

and

1. _____

See my _____ cat?

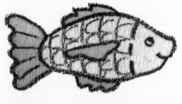 

2. _____

See my _____ cat?

3. _____

See my _____ cat?

4. _____

See my _____ cat.

THEME 5: Let's Count!
Week One
High-Frequency Word _and_

Children
- read the sentences and write _and_ to complete them
- mark smile (yes) or frown (no) to answer the questions
- draw the last picture

Home Connection
Let me read these sentences to you.

138

Name _____

THEME 5: Let's Count!
Week One _Feast for 10_
Categorize and Classify, Responding

Children
- color things they saw in the story _Feast for 10_
- draw foods in the cart they would buy for their own family's meal

 Home Connection
Today we heard a story called _Feast for 10_. Ask me to tell you about it.

139

Name _____

p   f   v

 | a | n

I see a bat _____ .

 | a | n

I see a _____ hat.

 | a | n

I see a cat _____ .

THEME 5: Let's Count!
Week One
Phonics: *p, -an*

140

Children
- write letters to complete the picture names (*pan*, *fan*, or *van*)
- write each word to complete the sentences

Home Connection
I can read these sentences. We can cut out the letter squares and build the words again. Then, we can make up some other silly hats.

Name _____

m	→	an	
v	→	an	
r	→	an	

A _____ sat.

A _____ .

A _____ ran.

THEME 5: Let's Count!
Week One
Phonics: -an Words

Children
• add letters to *-an* to build the words *man*, *van, ran*
• write these words to complete the sentences

Home Connection
Please listen to me read these words and sentences.

141

Name _____

| | **and   to   a** |

1.

I see a hat, _____

I like _____ see a hat.

2.

I like my hat.

3.

See my hat?

I see _____ hat I like.

4.

I like _____ see a hat.

Children
• read the sentences in the cartoon and write *and, to,* or *a* to complete them

 Home Connection
I'll read this cartoon to you. Then we can cut it apart to make a comic book.

Name _____

THEME 5: Let's Count!
Week Two _Counting Noodles_
Beginning/Middle/End

Children

1. think about the beginning of the story
2. finish the picture to show the middle of it
3. draw what the Noodles kept on doing at the end of the story

 Home Connection
Let me tell you the story, _Counting Noodles_. Then we can count the Noodle family.

Name _____

THEME 5: Let's Count!
Week Two *Counting Noodles*
Responding

Children
- think about a new story they might tell about the Noodles on a farm
- draw their ideas for their new story

 Home Connection
This is a picture for a story about the Noodles on a farm. Let me tell you about it.

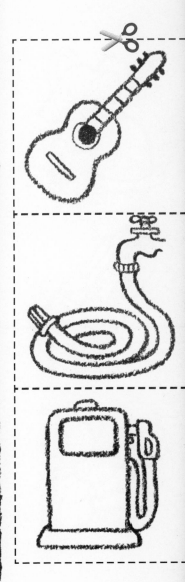

THEME 5: Let's Count!
Week Two
Phonemic Awareness: /g/

Children
- color all the pictures on pages 145 and 146 that start like *Gertie Goose*
- cut and paste the pictures for that sound in the boxes on page 146, then draw something else that starts with that sound

 Home Connection
Let's name all the things on the front and the back that start like Gertie Goose.

145

Name _____

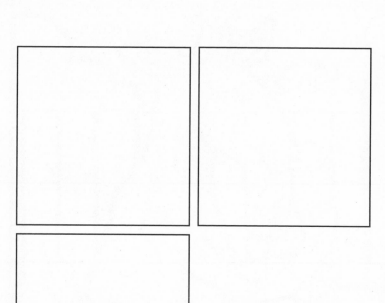

Name _____

1. ✏️

G g

2. g G g

Children
1. draw lines from pictures whose names start
   with the sound for g to the letters Gg
2. write Gg on the lines and draw something else
   that starts with the sound for g.

 Home Connection
Today we learned the letter g.
Help me find magazine pictures
whose names start with the
sound for g.

Name _____

van

go

bat

_____

- - - - - - - -

A van can _____ to a ▢.

A bat can _____ to a ▢.

THEME 5: Let's Count!
Week Two
High-Frequency Word *go*

Children
- read the sentences and write *go* to complete them
- complete the pictures for each sentence

Home Connection
I can read these sentences to you. Let's write *go*, *van*, and *bat*, then we can make up other sentences using these words.

148

Name _____

THEME 5: Let's Count!
Week Two *Ten Little Puppies*
Beginning/Middle/End, Responding

Children
1. count the puppies and draw more to show how many the boy had at the beginning
2. draw what one of the puppies did in the middle of the story

 Home Connection
Let me tell you the story *Ten Little Puppies*. Then I'll tell you about the pictures.

Name _____

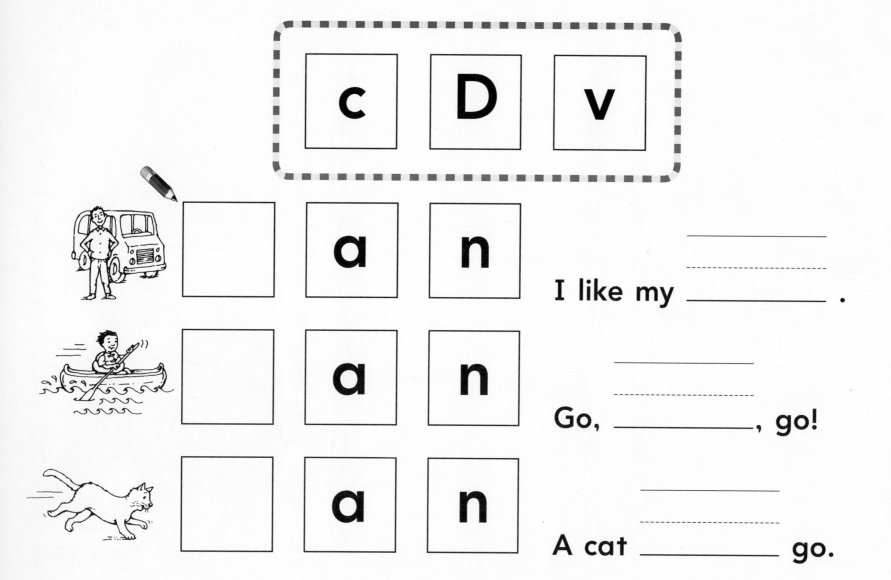

c D v

a n

I like my _____ .

a n

Go, _____, go!

a n

A cat _____ go.

THEME 5: Let's Count!
Week Two
Phonics: *g, -an*

Children
• write letters to complete the picture names *van*, *Dan*, and *can*
• write each word to finish the sentences

Home Connection
Let's cut out the letter squares, I'll read the sentences, then we can build *can*, *Dan*, and *van* again.

Name _____

THEME 5: Let's Count!
Week Three
Phonemic Awareness: /f/

Children

- color all the pictures on 155 and 156 that start like *Fifi Fish*
- cut and paste the pictures for that sound in the boxes on page 156
- draw something else that starts with that sound

 Home Connection
Let's name the things on the front and back that start like *Fifi Fish*.

Name _____

Name _____

1.

2.

3.

THEME 5: Let's Count!
Week Three *Feast for 10*
Categorize & Classify, Responding

Children
1. draw lines from things to eat you might get at the market to the cart
2. draw lines from things you would set the table with to the table
3. draw what you and your family might eat

 Home Connection
Let me tell you about this page and the special meal I drew.

157

Name _____

F f   F   —   f

5

4

THEME 5: Let's Count!
Week Three
Phonics: Initial Consonant _f_

Children
• write _Ff_ at the top
• name the pictures _Fifi Fish_ thinks about
• color and write _f_ beside pictures whose names begin with the sound for _f_

Home Connection
Today we learned the letter _f_. Help me find things around the house that start with the sound for _f_.

Name _____

I and go

1. _____

I sat _____ sat.

2. _____

Can I _____ ?

3. _____

_____ sat and sat.

4.

I can go!

THEME 5: Let's Count!
Week Three
High-Frequency Words Review and, go

Children
• Read the cartoon and write *I*, *and*, and *go* to complete what the fish says
• complete the picture for 4 to show how the fish will go

Home Connection
I can read this cartoon to you. What do you think comes to get the fish?

159

Name _____

f ➡ **an** _____

v ➡ **an** _____

c ➡ **an** _____

A _____ go.

I can _____ .

A _____ can go.

 THEME 5: Let's Count!
Week Three
Phonics: f, -an

Children
• add the letters to -an to build the words *fan*, *van*, and *can*
• write the words
• write each word to finish the sentences

Home Connection
We could cut the sentences into strips, and draw a picture to go with each.

Name _____

f	r	p

	a	n

I see a _____.

	a	n

A cat _____.

	a	n

See my _____ hat.

THEME 5: Let's Count!
Week Three
Phonics: *-an* Words

Children
• Add letters to write the words *fan*, *ran* and *pan*.
• Write words to complete the sentences

Home Connection
Let me read the sentences to you. Then we can cut out the letter squares, mix them up, and make the words again.

161

Name _____

and   go   a   to

1. _____

Can a cat _____ ?

☺ ☹

2. _____

Can _____ go?

☺ ☹

3. _____

A man _____ a cat can go.

☺ ☹

4.

I see a man and a .

THEME 5: Let's Count!
Week Three
High-Frequency Words Review and, go, a, to

Children
For 1, 2, 3,
- read the questions and write *and*, *go*, *a*, and *to* to complete them
- mark smile (yes) or frown (no) to show whether the pictures answer the questions

For 4, read the sentence and draw a picture to go with it

 Home Connection
Let me read these sentences to you. Then we can check to make sure the pictures go with the questions.

162

Name _____

Children

- color the pictures that show what might happen in a make-believe story but not in real life

- draw a picture of something that could happen in real life

 Home Connection
Let me tell you about the story *Chicken Soup with Rice* and why I colored the pictures that I did.

Name _____

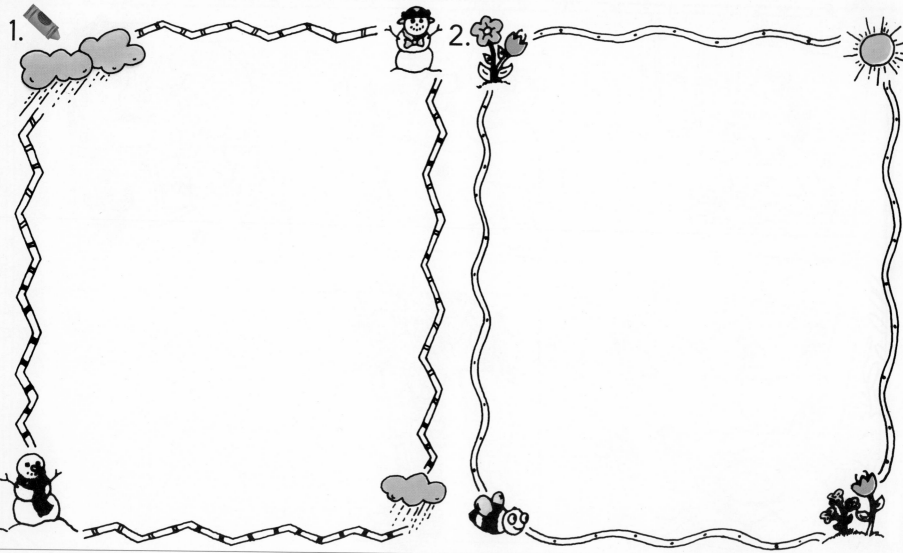

1.

2.

THEME 6: Sunshine and Raindrops
Week One _Chicken Soup with Rice_
Responding

Children

think of a favorite food they would like to eat all year long, in any kind of weather. Then they

1. draw themselves eating that food in hot weather

2. draw themselves eating that food in cold weather

 Home Connection

Let me tell you about some of the silly things a boy did in different months of the year in _Chicken Soup with Rice_. Then I'll tell you about the pictures I drew about a favorite food of mine.

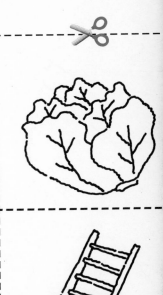

THEME 6: Sunshine and Raindrops
Week One
Phonemic Awareness: /l/

Children
- color all the pictures on pages 165 and 166 that start like *Larry Lion*
- cut and paste pictures for that sound in the boxes on page 166
- draw something else that starts with that sound

Home Connection
Let's name all the things on the front and back that start like *Larry Lion*.

165

Name _____

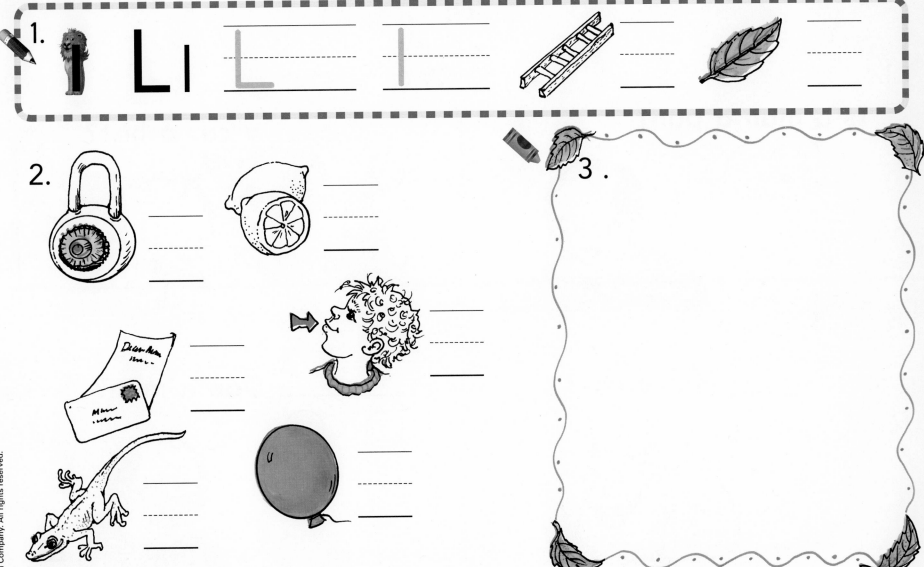

1. L L l ___ ___ ___

2.

3.

THEME 6: Sunshine and Raindrops
Week One
Phonics: Initial Consonant /

Children
- for 1 and 2, write *l* beside the pictures whose names start like *Larry Lion*
- for 3, draw two things whose names start with *l*

Home Connection
Would you help me find things in our house that start with the sound for *l*? Then we can make a list of what we find.

167

Name _____

 1.

Is a man a pan?

2. _____

_____

_____ **a cat a hat?**

3. _____

_____

_____ **Nat a cat?**

4. _____

_____

_____ **Dan a man?**

Is

THEME 6: Sunshine and Raindrops
Week One
High-Frequency Word: *is*

168

Children
- read the questions and look at the pictures
- write *Is* to complete 2, 3, and 4
- mark yes (smile) or no (frown) to show their answers to the questions

Home Connection
Ask me to read these questions to you. Then we can take turns asking other questions like these about things in this room.

Name _____

1.

2.

THEME 6: Sunshine and Raindrops
Week One *What Will the Weather Be Like Today?*
Fantasy/Realism, Responding

Children
1. color the picture that shows something that probably wouldn't happen in that kind of weather
2. draw something they themselves would do in the kind of weather shown

Home Connection
My teacher read a book to us called *What Will the Weather Be Like Today?* Let me tell you what I learned about weather from it and about the pictures I colored and drew.

169

Name _____

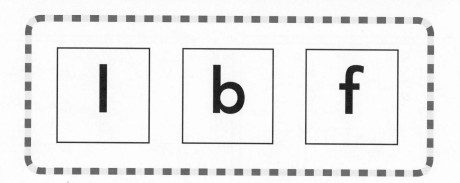

| l | b | f |

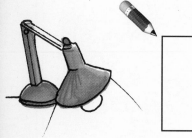

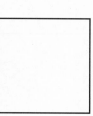 | i | t

| i | t

| i | t

 My  is _____ .

A cat can _____ .

A rat _____ my  .

 THEME 6: Sunshine and Raindrops
Week One
Phonics: *l, -it*

Children
- write the letters to complete the picture names (*lit*, *fit*, and *bit*)
- write each word to complete the sentences

 Home Connection
We can cut out the letter squares on this page, mix them up and unscramble them to build the words *lit*, *fit*, and *bit* again.

170

Name _____

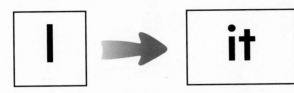

l → **it** _____

f → **it** _____

h → **it** _____

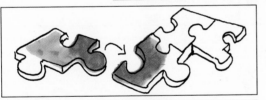

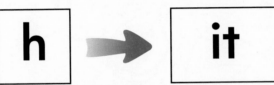

A 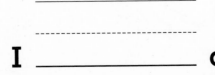 can _____.

A bat can _____.

I _____ a .

THEME 6: **Sunshine and Raindrops**
Week One
Phonics: -*it* **Words**

Children
- add letters to -*it* to build *lit*, *fit*, and *hit* and write the words
- write these words to complete the sentences that go with the pictures

 **Home Connection**
Ask me to read the sentences I finished to you. Then we can make up a silly sentence using the words I wrote.

171

Name _____

is   and   Go   see

1. and Cat see Rat.

I _____ Rat.

2. Is it Rat?

It _____ Rat.

3. Go _____ ! _____ Cat!

4. See _____ Cat go!

THEME 6: Sunshine and Raindrops
Week One
High-Frequency Words Review *is, and, go*

Children
• read the sentences in the cartoons and write words to complete them
• draw who Pig and Cat are running away from

 Home Connection
Let me read this cartoon to you. Then we can draw and write some more cartoon pictures together of something Pig, Cat, and Rat do.

Name _____

1.

2.

Theme 6: Sunshine and Raindrops
Week Two *The Sun and the Wind*
Plot

Children

1. draw what the man did when the wind blew harder and what he did when the sun got hotter

2. color the picture of the winner of the contest between the sun and the wind

 Home Connection
Let me tell you about what happened in a story I heard today called *The Sun and the Wind*.

173

Name _____

1.

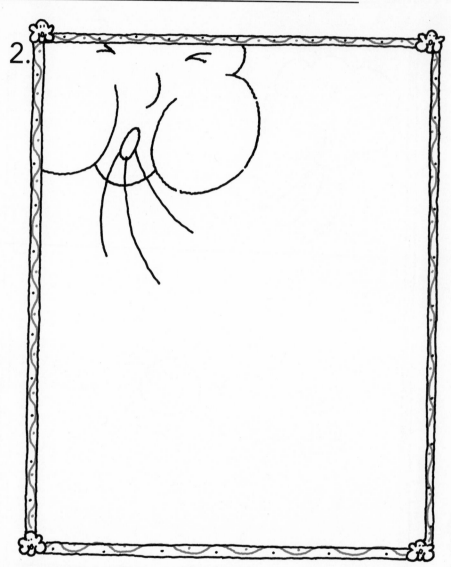

2.

THEME 6: Sunshine and Raindrops
Week Two *The Sun and the Wind*
Responding

Children
1. draw what they themselves would wear outside on a hot and sunny day and what they might do that day
2. draw what they themselves would wear outside on a very windy day and what they might do that day

 Home Connection
Let me tell you about the pictures I drew of myself in different kinds of weather.

174

Name _____

THEME 6: Sunshine and Raindrops
Week Two
Phonemic Awareness: /k/

Children
- color all the pictures on pages 175 and 176 that start like *Keeley Kangaroo*
- cut and paste pictures for that sound in the boxes on page 176
- draw something else that starts with that sound

Home Connection
Let's name all the things on the front and back that start like *Keeley Kangaroo.*

175

Name _____

Name _____

1.

Kk

2.

k Kk K _____ k

THEME 6: Sunshine and Raindrops
Week Two
Phonics: Initial Consonant _k_

Children
- draw lines from the pictures whose names start with the sound for _k_, to _Kk_
- write _Kk_ and draw something else for that sound in the box with Keely Kangaroo

 Home Connection
Let's look in story books to find some words that start with _k_. Every time we find one, you can read it and I'll write a _k_ on a list so we can count how many words we find.

177

Name _____

cat

rat

Here   here

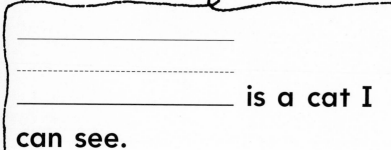

_____

_____ is a cat I

can see.

I can see a rat

_____

_____ .

THEME 6: Sunshine and Raindrops
Week Two
High-Frequency Word *here*

Children
- read the sentences and write *here* or *Here* to complete them
- draw a picture to go with each sentence

Home Connection
Ask me to read these sentences to you. Then I'll tell you about the pictures I drew to go with them.

Name _____

THEME 6: Sunshine and Raindrops
Week Two *All to Build a Snowman*
Plot, Responding

Children

1. think about what happened in the story as the children built their snowman
2. draw something funny that happened before they finished
3. draw things they themselves would have added to the snowman if they had been there to help build it

🏠 **Home Connection**
Let me tell you about the story *All to Build a Snowman*. It's about some funny things that happen when two children build a snowman.

179

Name _____

l	h	k

 | | i | t |  | A 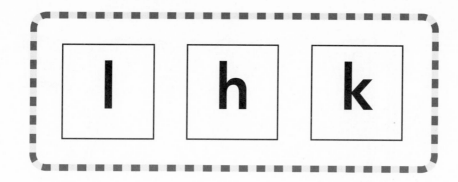 is _____ .

 | | i | t | I see a _____ .

 | | i | t | A man can _____ a .

 THEME 6: Sunshine and Raindrops
Week Two
Phonics: *k, -it*

Children
- write letters to complete the picture names (*lit*, *kit*, and *hit*)
- write each word to finish the sentences

 Home Connection
Let me read the sentences I finished with the words *lit*, *pit*, and *hit*. Then let's think of other sentences for these words. Will you write them for me?

Name _____

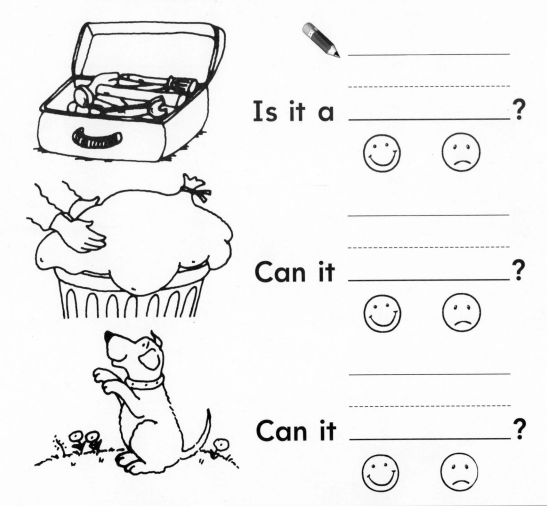

| sit | fit | kit |

Is it a _____?

😊   ☹

Can it _____?

😊   ☹

Can it _____?

😊   ☹

THEME 6: Sunshine and Raindrops
Week Two
Phonics: *-it* **Words**

Children
- read the questions and write words ending in
  -it to complete them
- mark the smile (yes) or the frown (no) to show
  whether the picture answers the question

 Home Connection
I can read these sentences to
you! Then we can write the
letters on separate scraps of
paper and build the words again.

181

Name _____

Here   is   and   go

1. _____

Here _____ my cat.

2. _____

_____ is my .

3. _____

See my cat _____ to a

4. _____

See my dog _____ my cat go!

THEME 6: Sunshine and Raindrops
Week Two
High-Frequency Words Review: *here, is, and, go*

182

Children
• read the sentences and write *Here, is, and,* and *go* to complete them
• complete the picture in box 4 to go with the sentence

Home Connection
Let me read you the sentences I finished and tell you about my picture.

Name _____

Theme 6: Sunshine and Raindrops
Week Three *The Woodcutter's Cap*
Fantasy/Realism

Children

1. color the animals that crawled into the cap in the story

2. draw a line from the animals they colored to the homes where these animals would live in real life

Home Connection
Let me tell you the make-believe story *The Woodcutter's Cap*. Then I'll tell you why this story could never happen in real life.

Name _____

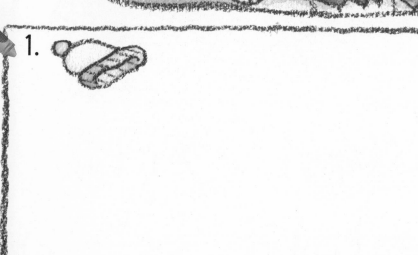

1.

2.

THEME 6: Sunshine and Raindrops
Week Three *The Woodcutter's Cap*
Responding

Children

1. think about and draw what would have happened if more animals had tried to squeeze into the cap before the bee came

2. think about and draw what would have happened if the man had found his cap when all the animals were still in it

Home Connection
I drew some pictures that show what might have happened in the story if some parts of it had been different. Listen and I'll tell you about my pictures and my ideas.

Name _____

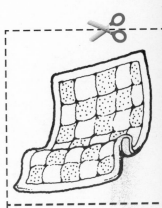

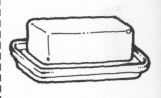

THEME 6: Sunshine and Raindrops
Week Three
Phonemic Awareness: /qu/

Children
- color all the pictures on pages 185 and 186 that start like *Queenie Queen*
- cut and paste the pictures for that sound in the boxes on page 186
- draw something else that starts with that sound

Home Connection
Let's name all the things on the front and back that start like *Queenie Queen.*

185

Name _____

Name _____

1. q Qu qu  Qu ___ qu ___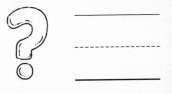

2.

 _____

 _____

 _____

 _____

3.

THEME 6: **Sunshine and Raindrops**
Week Three
Phonics: Initial Consonant *qu*

Children
- for 1 and 2, write *qu* beside the pictures whose names start like *Queenie Queen*
- for 3, draw a picture of something else whose name starts with *qu*

 Home Connection
Ask me to tell you about the pictures I wrote *qu* beside and about the picture I drew.

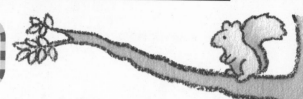

Is   here

1. _____
_ _ _ _ _ _ _ _ _ _ _ _ _

_____ my cat here?

2. _____

Is my cat _____?

3. _____
_ _ _ _ _ _ _ _ _ _ _ _ _

_____ my cat here?

4.

Here is my cat!

Children
• read the questions and write *Is* and *here* to complete them
• read the last sentence and draw the cat in the place where the child found it

 **Home Connection**
I finished the lines in this short story. Let me read it to you and tell you about the place the cat was hiding.

Name _____

1.

2.

THEME 6: Sunshine and Raindrops
Week Three _All to Build a Snowman_
Plot, Responding

Children

1. color the pictures that show something that happened in the story

2. draw two more things that they remember happened in the story

 Home Connection
We heard a story today called _All to Build a Snowman_. Ask me to tell it to you. I can point to the pictures as I tell that part.

189

Name _____

Can I _____ and sit?

A cat is at a _____ .

Can Rat _____?

 THEME 6: Sunshine and Raindrops
Week Three
Phonics: *qu, -it*

190

Children
- write letters to complete the words (*quit, pit, fit*)
- write each word to finish the sentences

 Home Connection
There aren't very many words that start with *qu*. Help me look in books for some and you can read me the ones we find.

Name _____

quit   sit   lit

_____
- - - - - - - - - -
See fox _____.

😊   ☹

_____
- - - - - - - - - -
Fox _____ a .

😊   ☹

_____
- - - - - - - - - -
Fox can _____.

😊   ☹

THEME 6: Sunshine and Raindrops
Week Three
Phonics: -it Words

Children
- read the sentences and write the words ending in -it to complete them
- mark the smile (yes) or the frown (no) to show whether the sentence goes with the picture

Home Connection
I've learned to read the words *quit*, *sit*, and *lit*. Let me read these sentences to you, then we can make up some silly rhymes with those words.

191

Name _____

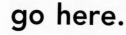

is   Here   and   go

1. _____

I like to _____ here.

2. _____

My cat _____ go here.   I like to

3. _____

My cat _____ here.

4. _____

_____ is my cat!

THEME 6: Sunshine and Raindrops
Week Three
High-Frequency Words Review *is,*
here, and, go

Children
- write *go, and, is,* and *Here* to complete what the cartoon character says
- draw the place the child wants the cat to go

Home Connection
Ask me to read the sentences in the speech balloons to you. Then we can think of other places the cat and child might like to go.

192

Name _____

1.

2.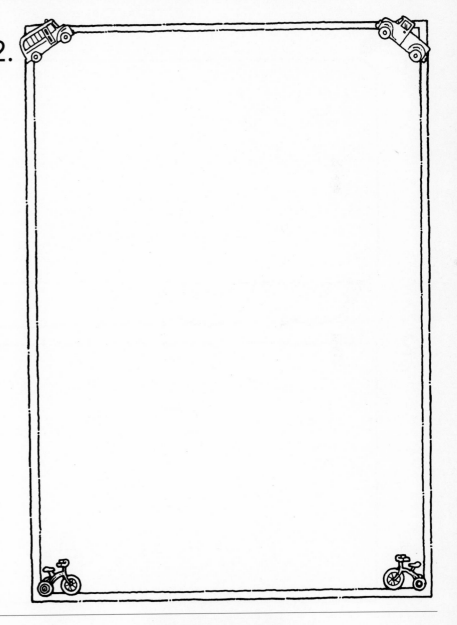

THEME 7: Wheels Go Around
Week One *Wheels Around*
Text Organization & Summarizing

Children
1. color the things with wheels and tell how wheels help those things do their jobs
2. draw something else that has wheels that they'd like to ride in

 Home Connection
I colored some things with wheels that my teacher read about today. Ask me how wheels help these things do their jobs.

193

Name _____

1.

2.

THEME 7: Wheels Go Around
Week One _Wheels Around_
Responding

Children
1. draw a picture on the side of the big truck to show what it is carrying
2. draw a picture to show where the big truck might be taking its load

 Home Connection
Next time we ride somewhere, we can watch for big trucks. Ask me what I'd haul if I had a truck.

194

THEME 7: Wheels Go Around
Week One
Phonemic Awareness: /d/

Children
- color all the pictures on pages 195 and 196 that start like *Dudley Duck*
- cut and paste pictures for that sound in the boxes on page 196
- draw something else that starts with that sound

 Home Connection
Let's name all the things on the front and back that start like *Dudley Duck*.

195

Name _____

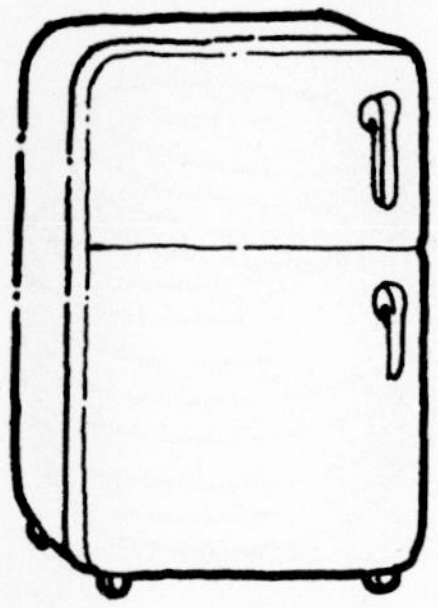

THEME 7: **Wheels Go Around**
Week One
Phonemic Awareness: /d/

Name _____

1.  **d Dd** D _____ d _____ 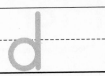 _____ _____

2.

3.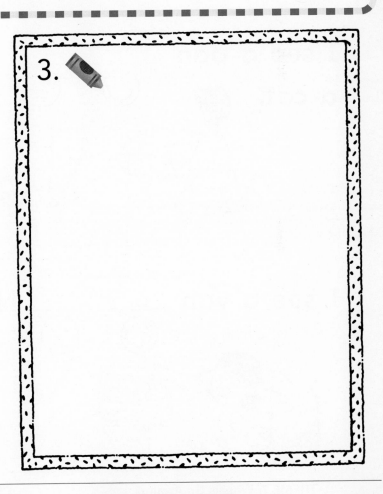

THEME 7: Wheels Go Around
Week One
Phonics: Initial Consonant _d_

Children
- for 1 and 2, practice writing _Dd_ and then write _d_ beside the pictures whose names start like _Dudley Duck_
- for 3, draw two things whose names begin with _d_

 Home Connection
Next time we watch TV together, let's see how many things beginning with _d_ we can find. Would you write what we find?

197

Name _____

for

1. _____

I see a pan _____ a cat.

2.

I see a mat and a hat
_____
_____ a man.

3. _____

I see a van _____ Nan.
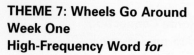

4. _____

I see a hat _____ Nan.

THEME 7: Wheels Go Around
Week One
High-Frequency Word *for*

Children
- for 1, 2, and 3, read the sentences and write the word *for* on the lines
- mark the smile (yes) or the frown (no) to show whether the picture goes with the sentence
- for 4, draw a hat for Nan and write the word *for*

Home Connection
I am learning to read the word *for*. Let me read these sentences to you. Then we could make up some more about Nan.

198

Name _____

THEME 7: Wheels Go Around
Week One *The Wheels on the Bus*
Organization & Summarizing, Responding

Children
- for 1–6, cross out things that didn't happen on the bus in the story
- for the empty box, draw something else that did happen in the story

Home Connection
I'll tell you what happened in the story *The Wheels on the Bus*. It's a song too, so if you know it, we can sing it together.

199

Name _____

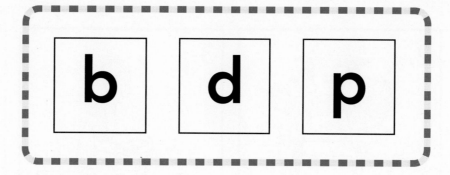

  **i** **g**

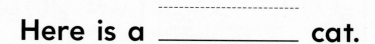
Here is a _____ cat.

  **i** **g**

A man can _____ .

   **i** **g**

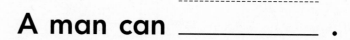
Is the _____ here?

 THEME 7: Wheels Go Around
Week One
Phonics: *d, -ig*

200

Children
- write the letters to complete the words *big*, *dig*, *pig*
- write each word to complete the sentences that go with the pictures

 Home Connection
Let's cut out the letter squares on this page, mix them up, and unscramble them to build the words *pig*, *dig*, and *big* again.

Name _____

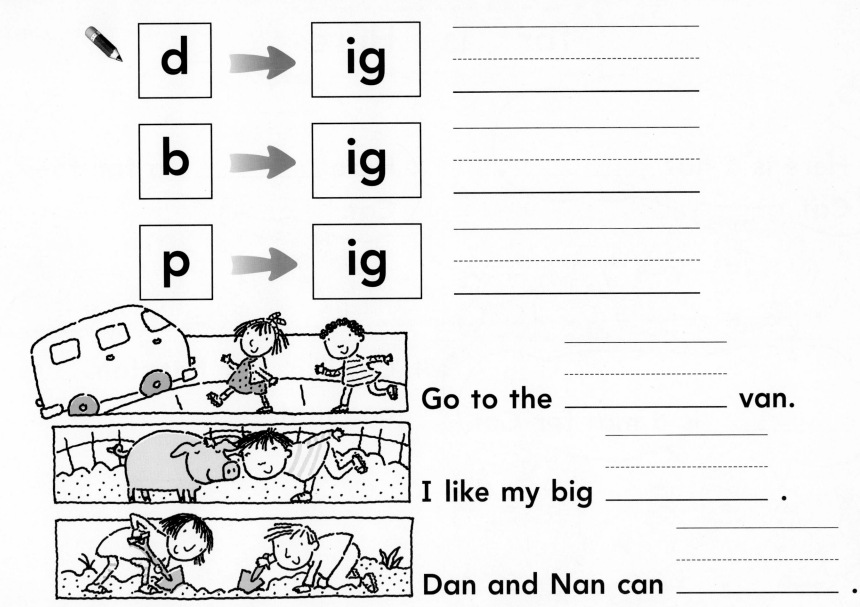

d → ig _____

b → ig _____

p → ig _____

Go to the _____ van.

I like my big _____ .

Dan and Nan can _____ .

THEME 7: Wheels Go Around
Week One
Phonics: -ig Words

Children
- add beginning letters to -ig to build dig, big, and pig
- write these words to complete the sentences that describe the pictures

 Home Connection
Please listen to me read these sentences. Then we can make up more sentences using the same words.

for   is   Here

1.
Here is a hat _____ Cat.

2. Here _____ a fan for Cat.

3. _____ is a mat for Cat.

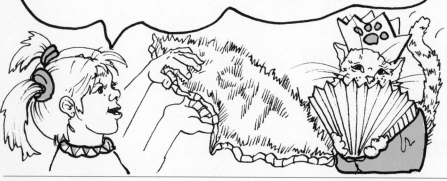

4. Cat likes her hat, fan, and mat.

THEME 7: Wheels Go Around
Week One
High-Frequency Words Review *for, is, here*

Children
- for 1, 2, and 3, write *for*, *is*, and *Here* to complete what the cartoon characters say
- for 4, draw a picture of Cat's mat, hat, and fan

Home Connection
Today I finished this cartoon.
Ask me to read it to you.

Name _____

1.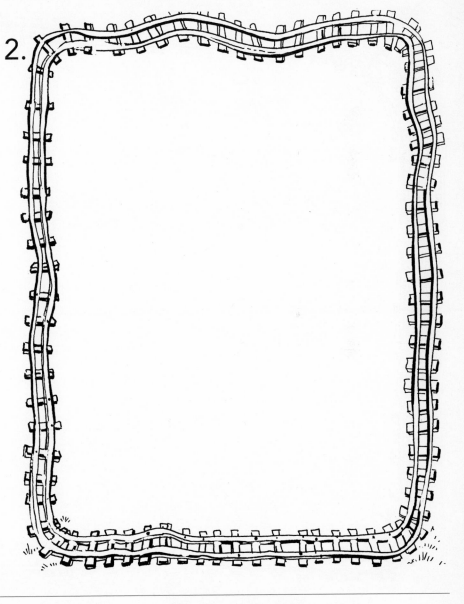

2.

THEME 7: Wheels Go Around
Week Two _The Little Engine That Could_
Cause and Effect

Children

1. think about what made the good little boys and girls happy at the end of the story and draw a picture to show that

2. draw something else they think would make the children happy

 Home Connection
Ask me to tell you about the picture I drew that shows why the children were happy at the end of the story _The Little Engine That Could._

203

Name _____

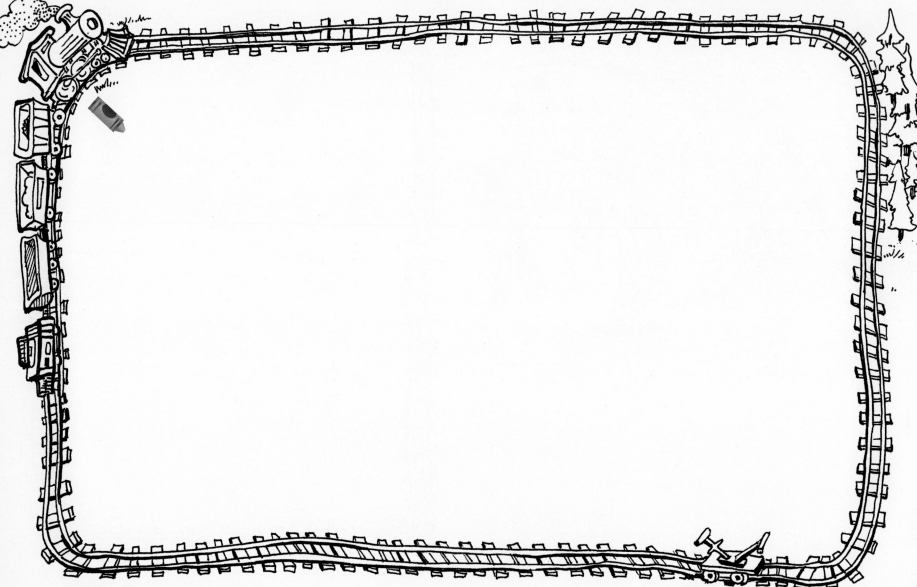

THEME 7: Wheels Go Around
Week Two *The Little Engine That Could*
Responding

Children
- think about the Little Engine in the story who tried very hard to pull a big load over the mountain
- draw a picture of something they themselves tried very hard to do

Home Connection
Ask me to tell you the story *The Little Engine That Could*. Then I'll tell you about something I tried very hard to do — just like the Little Engine in the story.

Name _____

THEME 7: Wheels Go Around
Week Two
Phonemic Awareness: /z/

Children
- color all the pictures on pages 205 and 206 that start like *Zelda Zebra*
- cut and paste pictures for that sound in the boxes on page 206
- draw something else that starts with that sound

Home Connection
Let's name all the things on the front and back that start like *Zelda Zebra*.

205

Name _____

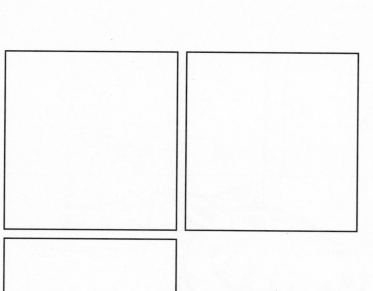

Name _____

1.

2.

Z z Z z _ _ Z _ _ z

THEME 7: Wheels Go Around
Week Two
Phonics: Initial Consonant z

Children
1. draw lines from pictures whose names start with the sound for z to the Zz
2. write Zz and draw something else for that sound in the box with *Zelda Zebra*

Home Connection

Let me tell you about the pictures I colored for the letter z and about the picture I drew. Then maybe you can help me write the name *Zelda Zebra*.

207

Name _____

have _____

_ _ _ _ _ _ _ _ _ _ _ _ _ _ _ _ _ _ _

_____

_____   _____

_ _ _ _ _ _ _ _ _ _ _ _ _ _ _ _ _ _ _   _ _ _ _ _ _ _ _ _ _ _ _ _ _ _ _ _ _ _

I _____ to sit here.   I _____ a pan.

_____   _____

_ _ _ _ _ _ _ _ _ _ _ _ _ _ _ _ _ _ _   _ _ _ _ _ _ _ _ _ _ _ _ _ _ _ _ _ _ _

I _____ to hit it.   I _____ a cat.

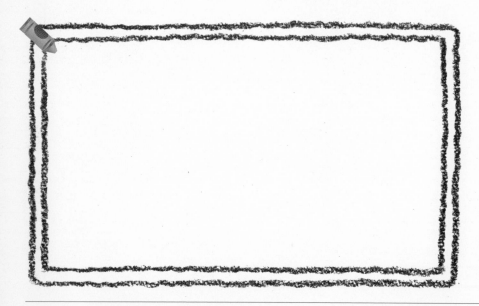

THEME 7: Wheels Go Around
Week Two
High-Frequency Word *have*

Children
- practice writing *have* on the lines at the top
- read the sentences above the boxes and write
  have to complete them
- choose and circle one sentence for each box
- draw a picture to go with it

Home Connection
Let me read these sentences to
you! I drew pictures to go with
two of the sentences. Let me tell
you about them.

208

Name _____

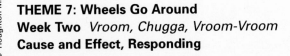

1.

2.

3.

THEME 7: Wheels Go Around
Week Two *Vroom, Chugga, Vroom-Vroom*
Cause and Effect, Responding

Children
- think what problem each of the race cars is having and what might have caused the problem
- draw their ideas for the cause of the problems shown in 1, 2, and 3

 Home Connection
Let me tell you about the story *Vroom, Chugga, Vroom-Vroom*. It's about a car race. All the cars had numbers. Have you ever been to or watched a car race? Tell me about it.

209

Name _____

Zig   dig   pig

 1. _____

My _____ is Zig.

2. _____

Zig can _____ .

3. _____

Here is my pig _____ .

 THEME 7: Wheels Go Around
Week Two
Phonics: z, -ig

Children
- read the sentences and write words ending in -ig to complete them
- mark the smile (yes) or the frown (no) to show whether the picture goes with the sentence beside it.

 Home Connection
Let me read these sentences to you! Then will you help me write the letters Z, i, d, p, and g on separate scraps of paper? We can build words with them.

Name _____

| z | b | p |

 **i** **g**

My cat _____ can dig.

 i **g**

My cat is a _____ cat.

 **i** **g**

My cat and my _____ like to sit.

THEME 7: Wheels Go Around
Week Two
Phonics: -ig Words

Children
- write letters to complete the words that go with the pictures (*Zig, big, pig*)
- write each word to finish the sentences

 Home Connection
Let me read you the sentences I finished with the words *Zig, big,* and *pig*. Then let's think of other sentences for these words. Will you write them for me?

211

Name _____

| have | for | is | Here |

1.

I _____ a big fig.

2.

Is it _____ Pig?

3.

It _____ for Pig and Cat.

4.

_____ is a big fig.

A big fig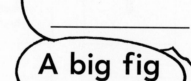

THEME 7: Wheels Go Around
Week Two
High-Frequency Words Review *have, for, is, here*

212

Children
• read the speech balloons
• write a word from the box to complete what the characters are saying
• color the pictures

Home Connection
Let me read this cartoon to you. Then maybe you can read a newspaper cartoon to me.

Name _____

1.

2.

THEME 7: Wheels Go Around
Week Three *Mr. Gumpy's Motor Car*
Making Predictions

Children
- think about what is happening in the pictures and predict what will happen to the man, his car, and the rabbits
- draw their predictions in the box under each picture

Home Connection
Let me tell you about the pictures I drew to show what I thought would happen next. Then let's talk about what else might happen for each picture.

213

Name _____

1.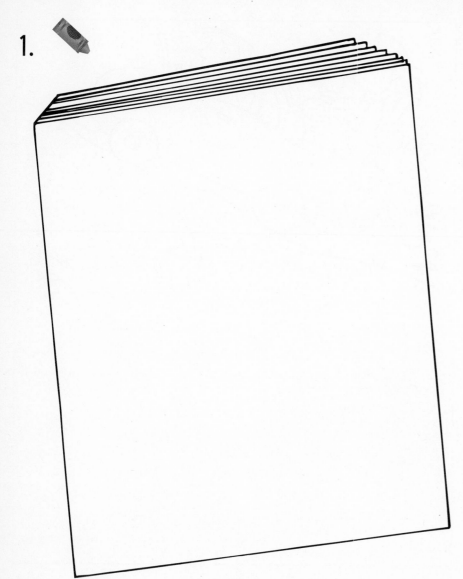

2.

THEME 7: Wheels Go Around
Week Three *Mr. Gumpy's Motor Car*
Responding

Children

1. think about what they would draw for the cover of the book *Mr. Gumpy's Motor Car* if they were the artist and draw it

2. draw a picture of themselves in the car when they're grown-up enough to drive

 Home Connection
Let me tell you about *Mr. Gumpy's Motor Car,* a funny story that my teacher read to us. Ask me to tell you about the pictures I drew.

Name _____

THEME 7: Wheels Go Around
Week Three
Phonemic Awareness Review: /d/, /z/

Children
for each row,
- color the Alphafriend and two things whose names begin like the Alphafriend *Dudley Duck* or *Zelda Zebra*
- draw something else that starts with the same sound

 Home Connection
Today I listened for words that start like *Dudley Duck* and *Zelda Zebra*. Ask me to tell you about the Alphafriends on this page and the pictures I colored.

215

Name _____

THEME 7: Wheels Go Around
Week Three
Phonemic Awareness Review: /d/, /z/

Children
- find and color two pictures that begin like *Dudley Duck*
- find and circle two pictures that begin like *Zelda Zebra*

Home Connection
Let's play a game. I'll look in a picture book for things whose names start like *Dudley Duck* and you can look for things that start like *Zelda Zebra*.

216

Name _____

THEME 7: Wheels Go Around
Week Three
Phonics Review: Initial Consonants *d, z*

Children
- use a yellow crayon to draw around *Dudley Duck* and to color all the pictures whose names begin with the sound for *d*
- use a blue crayon to draw around *Zelda Zebra* and to color all the pictures whose names begin with the sound for *z*
- write *d* beside yellow pictures and *z* beside blue pictures

 Home Connection
Today I colored pictures of things whose names begin with the sounds for *z* and *d*. Let me tell you about the blue and yellow pictures.

217

Name _____

for   have

1. _____

I _____ a hat for Nan.

2. _____

I have a bat _____ Nan.

3. _____

I _____ a van for Nan.

4. _____

I have a cat _____ Nan.

Children
- read the sentences and write *for* and *have* to complete them
- draw a picture to go with sentence 4

Home Connection
Today I wrote words and drew a picture to finish this short story. Let me read it to you.

Name _____

1.

2.

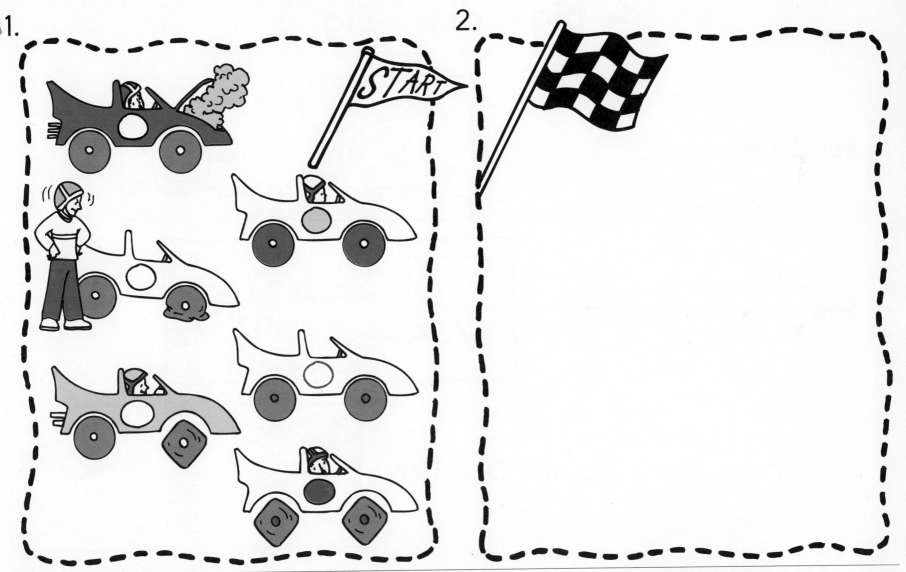

43180-T07W2-219A

THEME 7: Wheels Go Around
Week Three _Vroom, Chugga, Vroom-Vroom_
Making Predictions, Responding

Children
1. think about the troubles some of the race cars had in the story and color all the cars they think have a chance to win the race
2. draw a picture of the one car they predict will win

Home Connection
Let me tell you why I thought the car I drew would be the winner of this race. Which one do you think might win? Why?

219

big   dig   Zig

1. _____

See Dan _____ .

2. _____

See _____ dig.

3. _____

Can _____ Zig and Dan fit?

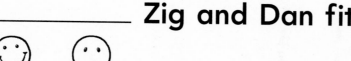

THEME 7: Wheels Go Around
Week Three
Phonics: *d, z, -ig*

Children
• read the sentences and write words ending in *-ig* to complete them
• mark the smile (yes) or the frown (no) to show whether the pictures go with the sentences

Home Connection
Let me read these sentences to you! Then will you help me write the letters *Z, i, d, b,* and *g* on separate scraps of paper? Then we can see how many words we can build with them.

220

Name _____

 b **z** **d**

 ☐ **i** **g**   Here is a _____ rig.

 ☐ **i** **g**   A big rig can _____ .

 ☐ **i** **g**   _____ can get a big rig to dig.

THEME 7: Wheels Go Around
Week Three
Phonics: -ig Words

Children
- write the letters to complete the words *big*, *dig*, and *Zig*
- write each word to complete the sentences that go with the pictures

 Home Connection
Let's look in a book together to find other words that end like *big* and *dig*. When we find them, would you help me read them?

Name _____

| have   for   is   Here |

1. _____

I have a hat _____
a man. ☺ ☹

2. _____

Here _____ a hat for
a  ☺ ☹

3. _____

I _____ a hat for a
☺ ☹

4. _____

_____ is a hat I like.

THEME 7: Wheels Go Around
Week Three
High-Frequency Words Review for, have, is, here

Children
• for 1, 2, and 3, read the sentences and write words to complete them,
• mark the smile (yes) or frown (no) to show whether the sentences go with the pictures
• for 4, read the sentence and draw a hat they like

Home Connection
I wrote *have, for, is,* and *here* to finish the sentences. Let me read them to you, and tell you about my picture.

222

Name _____

1.

2.

THEME 8: Down on the Farm
Week One *The Story of Half-Chicken*
Fantasy/Realism

Children
for each box,
- decide which pictures show things that could really happen and which show things that could never happen in real life
- color the two pictures of things that could really happen

 Home Connection
Ask me to tell you about these pictures. I'll tell you why I think the ones I didn't color are make-believe and could never happen in real life.

Name _____

1.

2.

3.

THEME 8: Down on the Farm
Week One *The Story of Half-Chicken*
Responding

224

Children

1. draw a picture of themselves meeting Half-Chicken on his way to the palace

2. draw a picture of Half-Chicken helping them in some way

3. draw a picture of something they would do to help Half-Chicken

 Home Connection
Let me tell you a story I heard today about a special chicken. He was called Half-Chicken. Then I'll tell you about the pictures I drew.

Name _____

1.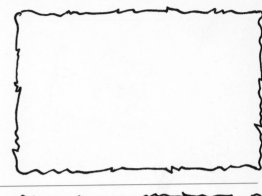

2.

3.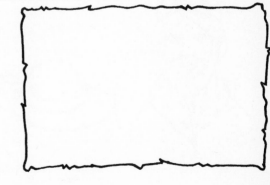

THEME 8: Down on the Farm
Week One
Phonemic Awareness Review: /t/, /k/, /n/

Children
for each row,
- color the Alphafriend and two pictures whose names start like that Alphafriend's name
- draw something else whose name starts with the same sound

 Home Connection
Let me tell you about these Alphafriends and the pictures I colored and drew in each row.

225

Name _____

1.

2.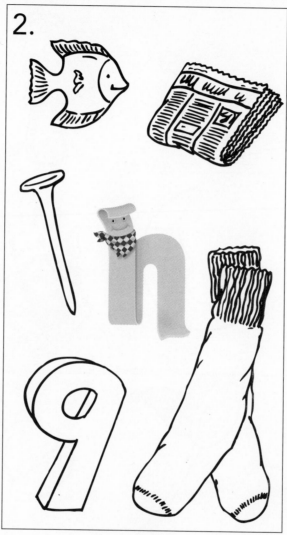

3.

THEME 8: Down on the Farm
Week One
Phonemic Awareness Review: /t/, /k/, /n/

Children
for each box,
- name the Alphafriend and the pictures
- color the pictures that have the same beginning sound as the Alphafriend
- draw lines to connect the pictures they colored with the Alphafriend

 Home Connection
Let's find magazine pictures whose names start like *Tiggy Tiger, Keely Kangaroo,* and *Nyle Noodle.*

Name _____

 T 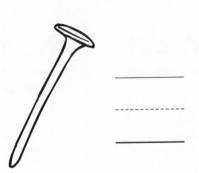 K k 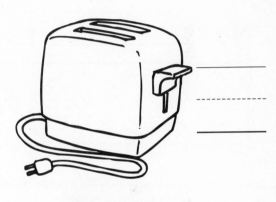 n N n

THEME 8: Down on the Farm
Week One
Phonics Review: Initial Consonants *t, k, n*

Children
- name each Alphafriend and letters at the top
- write the letters *Tt, Kk, Nn*
- color the pictures and write the letter for the sound they hear at the beginning of each picture

 Home Connection
Let's see how many things we can find that begin with the sounds for *t, k,* or *n*. Will you write down what we find? Then I'll check to make sure they start with one of these letters.

227

Name _____

said

1. _____

Nat _____ to fan a cat.

😊 ☹️

2. _____

Nan _____ to fan a pig.

😊 ☹️

3. _____

Dan _____ to fan a rat.

😊 ☹️

4. _____

I _____, "Fan a rat?"

THEME 8: Down on the Farm
Week One
High-Frequency Word *said*

Children
- write the word *said* to complete each sentence
- read the sentences
- mark the smile (yes) or the frown (no) to tell whether the picture goes with the sentence

 Home Connection
I'm learning to read the word *said*. Let me read this cartoon to you.

228

Name _____

1.

2.

3.

4.

THEME 8: Down on the Farm
Week One *Cows in the Kitchen*
Fantasy/Realism, Responding

Children
for each box,
- decide which picture shows something silly that real cows, ducks, pigs, and chickens couldn't do in real life and color that picture

 Home Connection
Let me tell you about some farm animals that caused trouble in the story *Cows in the Kitchen*. Then we can make up some more parts for the story.

229

Name _____

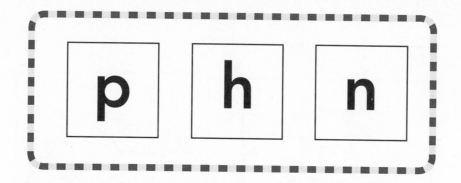

o | t

My _____ is not big.

o | t

My pot is _____ .

o | t

My pot is _____ for a cat.

 THEME 8: Down on the Farm
Week One
Phonics: *n, -ot*

Children
- write letters to complete the picture names *pot*, *hot*, and *not*
- read the sentences and write the words to complete them

 Home Connection
Let's cut out the letter squares on this page, mix them up, and unscramble them. Then we can make the words *pot*, *hot*, and *not* again.

230

Name _____

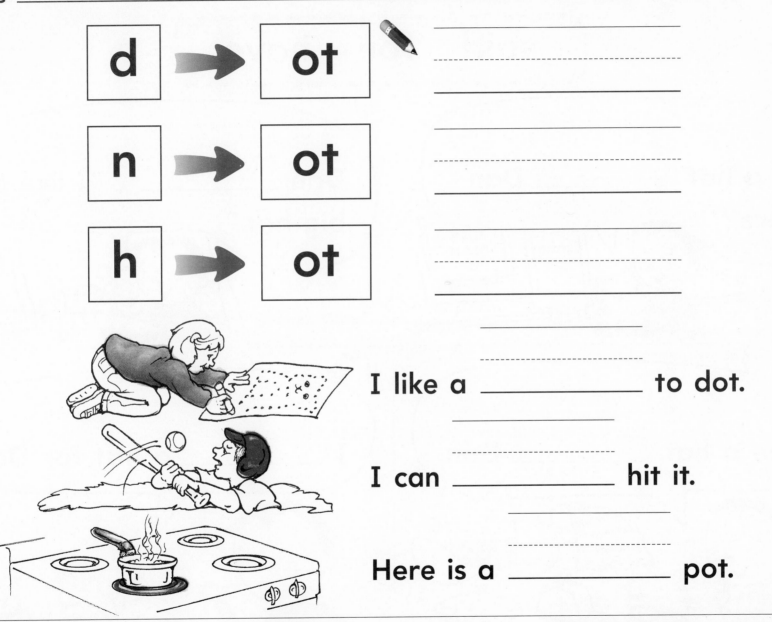

d ➡ ot

n ➡ ot

h ➡ ot

I like a _____ to dot.

I can _____ hit it.

Here is a _____ pot.

Children
• blend and write the words *dot, not, hot*
• read the sentences about the pictures and write words to complete them

 Home Connection
Would you like to help me read these sentences? Then we can make up other sentences using *dot, not,* and *hot.*

231

Name _____

said   for   have

1. Is a hat _____ Dan here?

2. Dan _____ , "I like a big hat."

3. See a hat _____ Dan.

4. I _____ a hat for Dan.

THEME 8: Down on the Farm
Week One
High-Frequency Words Review said, for, have

Children
• write the words to complete the sentences
• draw Dan's hat on the cat

Home Connection
Ask me to read this cartoon to you. Then I'll tell you about the hat for Dan that I drew.

Name _____

THEME 8: Down on the Farm
Week Two *The Enormous Turnip*
Noting Important Details

Children
- color who came to help when the grandfather called
- color who came to help when the grand-daughter called
- draw a picture of who came last to help pull up the turnip

 Home Connection
We heard a story called *The Enormous Turnip*. Do you know this story? Let me tell you who was in it and what happened.

233

Name _____

1.

2.

THEME 8: Down on the Farm
Week Two *The Enormous Turnip*
Responding

Children

- think about how the story would have been different (1) if no one had been around to help the farmer pull up the big turnip or (2) if the turnip hadn't been very big at all

- draw their ideas

 Home Connection
Ask me to tell you about the pictures I drew that show my ideas for two different stories about pulling up a turnip.

234

Name _____

THEME 8: Down on the Farm
Week Two
**Phonemic Awareness: /x/ in
Final Position**

Children

- color all the pictures on pages 235 and 236 that end in the sound they hear in *Mr. X-Ray*

- cut and paste the pictures for that sound in the boxes on page 236

- draw a picture of something else that ends with that sound

Home Connection
Today I listened for words that end with the sound I can hear in *Mr. X-Ray*. Let me tell you what they are.

235

Name _____

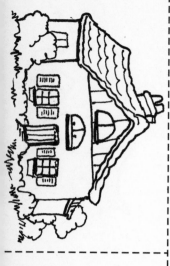

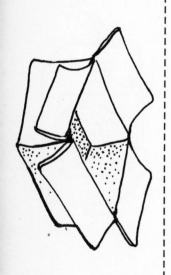

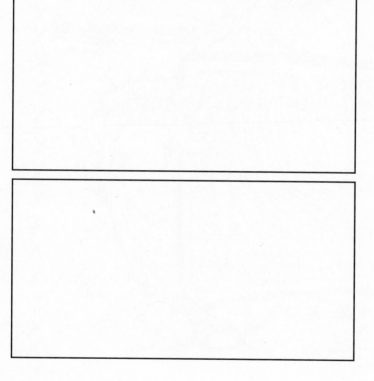

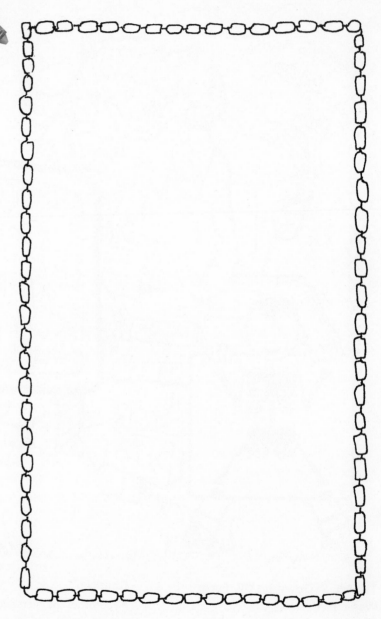

Name _____

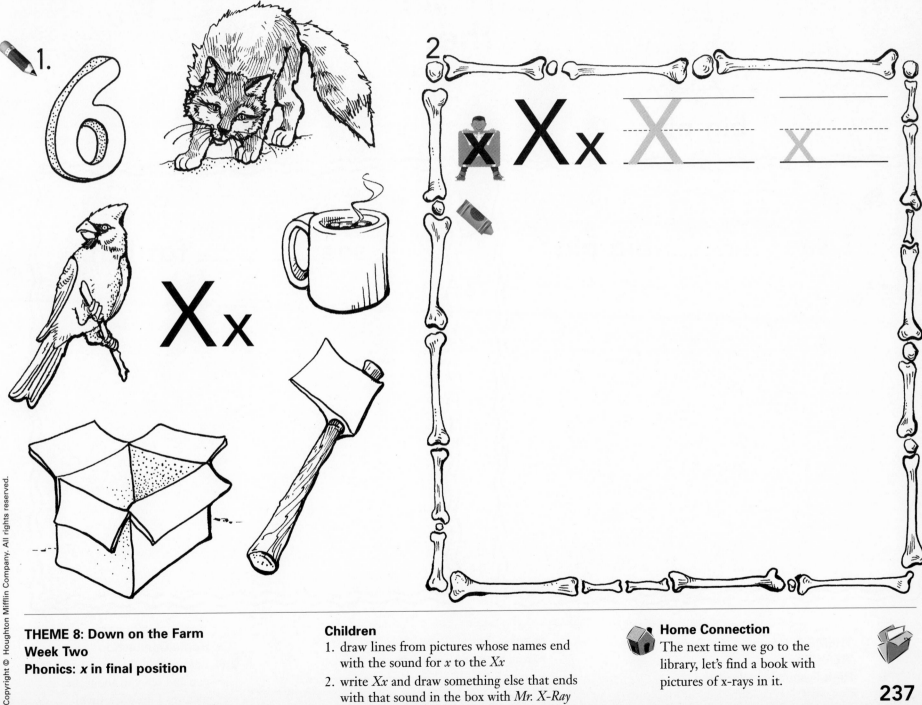

THEME 8: Down on the Farm
Week Two
Phonics: *x* in final position

Children
1. draw lines from pictures whose names end with the sound for *x* to the *Xx*
2. write *Xx* and draw something else that ends with that sound in the box with *Mr. X-Ray*

Home Connection
The next time we go to the library, let's find a book with pictures of x-rays in it.

237

Name _____

big pig

the

fat bat

_____
- - - - - - - - - - -
I see _____ big pig.

_____
- - - - - - - - - - -
I see _____ fat bat.

Children
- read the word and the sentences
- write the word to complete the sentences
- draw a picture for each sentence

 Home Connection
Let me read these sentences to you and tell you about the pictures I drew for them.

Name _____

1.

2.

3.

4.

THEME 8: Down on the Farm
Week Two _Mouse's Birthday_
Noting Important Details, Responding

Children
- for 1, 2, 3, draw pictures of what Mouse might do with each of these birthday gifts
- for 4, draw a picture of what they would like to give Mouse and what Mouse would probably do with that gift

 Home Connection
Let me tell you the story my teacher read to us today. It's _Mouse's Birthday_. Then I'll tell you about the gifts Mouse got and what I would give him.

239

Name _____

 **fox   box**

1. **See my** _____ **?**

2. **Is my** _____ **big?**

3. **Is it a box for my** _____ **?**

THEME 8: Down on the Farm
Week Two
Phonics: -ox Words

Children
- read the sentences and write words ending in -ox to complete them
- mark the smile (yes) or the frown (no) to show whether the pictures answer the questions

 Home Connection
Let me read these questions to you. We can cut out the words at the top into separate letters, scramble them, and build the words again.

Name _____

b f

o x

o x

Fox ran to a big _____ .

See _____ go to the box and sit.

THEME 8: Down on the Farm
Week Two
Phonics: -ox words

Children
• write letters to complete the picture names (*box* and *fox*)
• write each word to complete the sentences

 Home Connection
Ask me to read these sentences to you. Then let's take turns making up other things Fox could do with a box.

241

Name _____

the   said

1. _____

"I see _____ fox," said
Pig.

2. _____

"I see the pig," _____
Fox.

3. _____

"I see a box," _____
the pig.

4. The fox can not see

_____ pig.

**THEME 8: Down on the Farm
Week Two
High-Frequency Words Review *the, said***

242

Children
- read the cartoon sentences and write *the* and *said* to complete them
- draw the pig in the place he is hiding for the last sentence

 Home Connection
Ask me to read this cartoon to you. Then I'll tell you about why Fox couldn't see the pig.

Name _____

1.

2.

3.

THEME 8: Down on the Farm
Week Three *A Lion on the Path*
Drawing Conclusions

Children
- for 1 and 2, color the picture of what the cat or the rabbit is trying to get away from
- for 3, draw a picture of what they themselves might run away from

Home Connection
The story *A Lion on the Path* is about a farmer who gets away from a lion by tricking it. Let me tell you how he did that.

243

Name _____

1.

2.

THEME 8: Down on the Farm
Week Three *A Lion on the Path*
Responding

Children
1. think about what the rabbit in the story might do after it jumps into its hole and draw a picture of their idea
2. think about what the lion in the story might do after the rabbit gets away and draw a picture of their idea

 Home Connection
I made up more for the story *A Lion on the Path* and I drew pictures. Let me tell you about my pictures.

Name _____

1.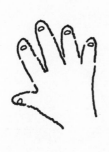

2.

3.

THEME 8: Down on the Farm
Week Three
Phonemic Awareness Review: /h/, /f/, /s/

Children
for each row,
- color the Alphafriend and two pictures whose names start like the Alphafriend's name (*Hattie Horse*, *Fifi Fish*, or *Sammy Seal*)
- draw another picture at the end of the row that starts with the same sound

Home Connection
Let me tell you about these Alphafriends and why I colored the pictures beside them. Then I'll tell you about the pictures I drew.

245

Name _____

THEME 8: Down on the Farm
Week Three
Phonemic Awareness Review: /h/, /f/, /s/

Children
color the pictures and
- draw lines from *Fifi Fish* to the things that start like her name
- draw lines from *Hattie Horse* to the things that start like her name
- draw lines from *Sammy Seal* to the things that start like his name

 Home Connection
Please help me find pictures in books and magazines of some things that start like *Hattie Horse*, *Fifi Fish*, and *Sammy Seal*.

Name _____

  F f _____ h H h _____ s S s _____

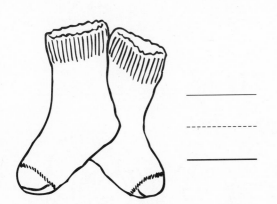  

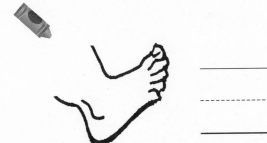  

THEME 8: Down on the Farm
Week Three
Phonics Review: Initial Consonants _h, f, s_

Children
- name each Alphafriend and letters at the top
- write the letters _Hh, Ff_, and _Ss_
- color the pictures and write the letter for the sound they hear at the beginning of each picture

 Home Connection
Please help me write the letters _h, f,_ and _s._ Then we can hunt for things or pictures whose names begin with the sounds for these letters.

Name _____

said   the

1. _____

"I have _____ box," said Nan.

2. _____

"Here is my cat," _____ Nan.

3. _____

"I like the box," _____ the cat.

4. _____

Nan said, "It is _____ box for my cat."

**THEME 8: Down on the Farm
Week Three
High-Frequency Words Review *said, the***

Children
- read the sentences and write *said* or *the* to complete them
- color the pictures

Home Connection
Ask me to read this short story to you. Then we can look through some books together to find the words *said* and *the*.

248

Name _____

1.

2.

THEME 8: Down on the Farm
Week Three *Mouse's Birthday*
Drawing Conclusions, Responding

Children

1. draw some of the guests and something that happened at Mouse's party

2. draw some guests that might come to a party for the farmer and what might happen at that party

 Home Connection
We heard a story today about a mouse's birthday party. Let me tell you the funny things that happened and about the pictures I drew.

249

Name _____

See   fox   hot

1. _____

See the fat _____ ?

2. _____

_____ the pig?

3. _____

See the _____ fox?

THEME 8: Down on the Farm
Week Three
Phonics Review: *s, f, h, -ot, -ox*

250

Children
- read the questions and write *See*, *fox* and *hot* to complete them
- mark yes (smile) or no (frown) to show whether the pictures answer the questions

 Home Connection
Let me read these questions to you. Then we can cut the sentences into separate words, scramble them, and build the sentences again.

Name _____

| h | f | b |

| | o | t |

I have a _____ pot.

| | o | x |

My _____ can go to the van.

| | o | x |

The big _____ ran to the van.

THEME 8: Down on the Farm
Week Three
Phonics Review: -ot, -ox Words

Children
• write letters to complete the picture names *hot*, *box*, and *fox*
• write each word to finish the sentences

 Home Connection
Ask me to read the words and the sentences to you. Then let's try to say "Do not put the fox in the box with the pot" very fast five times. Do you think we can do that without laughing?

251

Name _____

> said   the   for   have

1.

Nat said, "Here is the fox

_____
- - - - - - - - - - - - - - - - -
_____ Dan."

2.

_____
- - - - - - - - - - - - -

Dot _____ , "I have the
pig for Dan."

3.

Nan said, "Here is

_____
- - - - - - - - - - - - - - - - -
_____ cat for Dan."

4.

_____
- - - - - - - - - - - -

"I _____ the van

- - - - - - - - - - - -
_____ Dan."

THEME 8: Down on the Farm
Week Three
High-Frequency Words Review *said, the,*
for, have

Children
- read the words at the top
- read the sentences and write the words to complete them
- color the picture of the gift for Dan they like best

Home Connection
I've learned to read the words *said, the, for,* and *have*. Let me read you the sentences that have these words in them.

Name _____

1 2 3

THEME 9: Spring Is Here
Week One *Kevin and His Dad*
Sequence of Events

Children
- write 1, 2, and 3 in the pictures to show what Kevin and his dad did first, next, and last in the story
- color the pictures that show the boy and his dad working

 Home Connection
Ask me to tell you the story we heard today, *Kevin and His Dad*. Then we can talk about what steps we need to take to do a job at home together.

253

Name _____

THEME 9: Spring Is Here
Week One _Kevin and His Dad_
Responding

Children
- draw themselves doing a chore with a family member
- draw some objects they might use for doing different chores around home

 Home Connection
Let me tell you about the pictures I drew. Let's see how many of our chores are like the ones Kevin did with his dad.

Name _____

THEME 9: Spring Is Here
Week One
Phonemic Awareness: /w/

Children
- color all the pictures on pages 255 and 256 that start like *Willy Worm*
- cut and paste the pictures for that sound in the boxes on page 256
- draw something else that starts with that sound

Home Connection
Let's name some things around the house that start like *Willy Worm*.

255

Name _____

THEME 9: Spring Is Here
Week One
Phonemic Awareness: /w/

Name _____

1. W w _____ W _____ W _____ _____ _____

2. _____

3.

THEME 9: Spring Is Here
Week One
Phonics: Initial Consonant *w*

Children
For 1 and 2, children write *w* beside the pictures
whose names start like *Willy Worm*
For 3, children draw two things whose names
start with *w*

 Home Connection
Today we learned the letter *w*.
Let's look through magazines for
pictures whose names begin with
that sound. You can help me
make a list of the things we find.

257

Name _____

play

1. _____

Dan can _____ .

2. _____

Nan can not _____ .

3. _____

Pat can _____ .

4. _____

Can Nat _____ ?

THEME 9: Spring Is Here
Week One
High-Frequency Word *play*

258

Children
- read the sentences and write *play* to complete them
- mark the smile (yes) or the frown (no) to show whether the pictures go with the sentences
- draw a picture for sentence 4

Home Connection
Let me read these sentences to you. Then I'll tell you about the pictures I drew.

Name _____

1 2 3

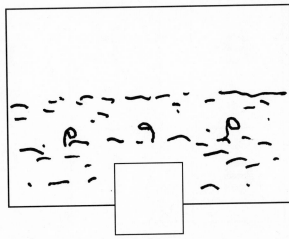

THEME 9: Spring Is Here
Week One
Sequence of Events

Children
For each row,
- write 1, 2, 3 below each picture to show what happens first, next, and last
- color the pictures that show what happens last
- think of a story for each row of pictures

 Home Connection
I wrote 1, 2, and 3 on the pictures to show what happens first, next, and last. Let me tell you a story I thought of for each row.

259

Name _____

w	s	p

| | e | t |

Do not let the cat

_____

get _____.

| | e | t |

I can _____
the hot pan here.

| | e | t |

Can I have a pig

_____

for a _____?

THEME 9: Spring Is Here
Week One
Phonics: *w, -et*

Children
• write the letters to complete the picture names (*wet*, *set*, and *pet*)
• write each word to complete the sentences that go with the pictures

 Home Connection
Let me read these sentences to you. We can cut the letters apart to build *wet*, *set*, and *pet* again.

260

Name _____

| v | → | et |

_____
- -
_____

| y | → | et |

_____
- -
_____

| g | → | et |

_____
- -
_____

_____
- -

Can you _____ to the cat?

- -

The _____ can see my pet.

- -

I can not see Nan _____ .

THEME 9: Spring Is Here
Week One
Phonics: -et Words

Children
- add the beginning letters to -et and write *vet*, *yet*, and *get*
- write these words to complete the sentences that describe the pictures

 Home Connection
Ask me to read these sentences to you. Then help me think of some more words that end in -et, like the words I wrote.

Name _____

1. _____

"I can play," _____
the cat.

2. _____

"I can _____ ,"
said the pig.

3.

"I can not play," _____

said _____ fox.

4.

See the cat and the pig
play.

THEME 9: Spring Is Here
Week One
High-Frequency Words Review *play, said, the*

Children
- read the sentences and write *play, said,* or *the* to complete them
- draw a picture to go with sentence 4

Home Connection
Listen to me read this cartoon. Then we can cut it apart and put it together like a book. After we make a cover for it, I can read it to someone else.

262

Name _____

1.

2.

THEME 9: Spring Is Here
Week Two *The Tortoise and the Hare*
Characters/Setting

Children

1. circle the pictures that show who the story was about

2. color the picture that shows where the story happened

 Home Connection
Ask me to tell you the story, *The Tortoise and the Hare*. Then I'll tell you about the pictures of who was in the story and where it all happened.

263

Name _____

 1.

2.

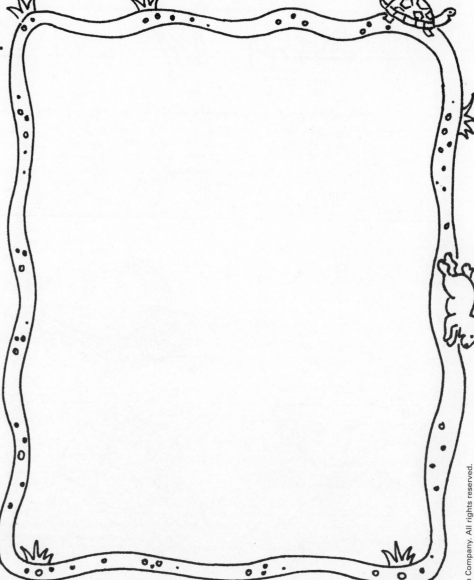

THEME 9: Spring Is Here
Week Two *The Tortoise and the Hare*
Responding

Children

1. choose and color a character Hare might want to race with the next time
2. draw their own picture of this new race

 Home Connection
While you're looking at my picture, I'll tell you about who is in my story about a race and where the race might take place.

264

Name _____

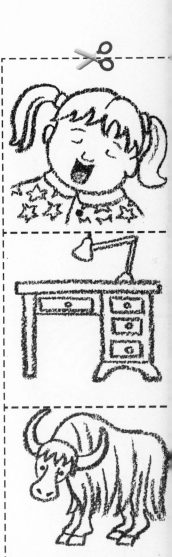

THEME 9: Spring Is Here
Week Two
Phonemic Awareness: /y/

Children

- color all the pictures on pages 265 and 266 that start like *Yetta Yo-Yo*
- cut and paste pictures for that sound in the boxes on page 266
- draw something else that starts with that sound

Home Connection

Let me tell you which pictures start like *Yetta Yo-Yo*. Then we can look around the house for yellow things — *yellow* starts like *Yetta Yo-Yo*.

265

Name _____

Name _____

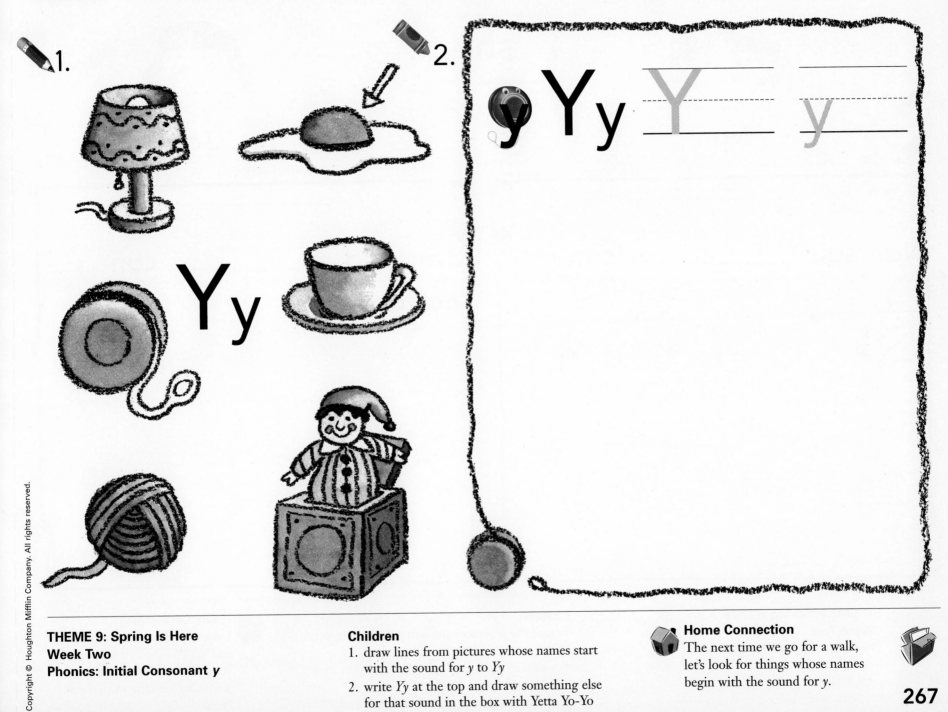

1.

2.

Y y

THEME 9: Spring Is Here
Week Two
Phonics: Initial Consonant _y_

Children
1. draw lines from pictures whose names start with the sound for _y_ to _Yy_
2. write _Yy_ at the top and draw something else for that sound in the box with Yetta Yo-Yo

 Home Connection
The next time we go for a walk, let's look for things whose names begin with the sound for _y_.

Name _____

Nan

she

Jan

Nan said _____ can go.

Jan said _____ can not go.

THEME 9: Spring Is Here
Week Two
High-Frequency Word *she*

Children
- read the sentences and write *she* to complete them
- complete the face pictures at the top to show how each girl feels
- draw a picture to go with each sentence

Home Connection
I can read these sentences to you and tell you about the pictures I drew. Then let's think of other sentences with the word *she* in them.

Name _____

THEME 9: Spring Is Here
Week Two *Mrs. McNosh Hangs Up Her Wash*
Characters/Setting, Responding

Children
- draw the person this story is about
- draw some things she hung on her clothesline and some of the things she saw around her clothesline as she worked

 Home Connection
Would you like me to tell you a funny story I heard today? It's called *Mrs. McNosh Hangs Up Her Wash*. Can you guess who the story is about?

269

Name _____

hen   ten   pen

1. _____

   Can a _____ fit here?

   ☺   ☹

2. _____

   Can  _____ fit here?

   ☺   ☹

3. _____

   Can the _____ fit here?

   ☺   ☹

THEME 9: Spring Is Here
Week Two
Phonics: -en Words

Children
- read the questions and write -en words to complete them
- mark the smile (yes) or the frown (no) to show their answers to the questions about the pictures

Home Connection
Let's write *hen*, *ten*, and *pen* on a piece of paper. Then I'll make up sentences with these words and you can write my sentences.

270

Name _____

| h | p | m |

☐ **e** **n** I see the _____.

☐ **e** **n** The _____ sat and sat.

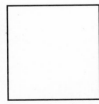

☐ **e** **n** Nan and Dan have the
_____.

THEME 9: Spring Is Here
Week Two
Phonics: *-en* Words

Children
- write letters to complete the picture names (*men*, *hen*, and *pen*)
- write each word to finish the sentences

 Home Connection
Let's cut out the letter squares, mix them up, and build the words *hen*, *pen*, and *men* again. Can you help me make up other sentences with these words?

271

Name _____

she   said   play   the

1. _____

"I can play it," _____

said.

2. _____

"I can _____ it,"

she said.

3. _____

She _____, "I can

play the  ."

4. _____

And I said, "I can play

_____

_____

_____

THEME 9: Spring Is Here
Week Three
High-Frequency Words Review she, play, said, the

272

Children
• for 1 and 2, read the sentences and write *she*, *said*, and *play* to complete them
• for 4, write *the* and draw a picture to finish the sentence

 Home Connection
Ask me to read these sentences to you. Then I can tell you about the picture I drew in 4.

Name _____

THEME 9: Spring Is Here
Week Three *The Three Billy Goats Gruff*
Categorize and Classify

Children
- color yellow the things for Little Billy Goat, red for Middle Billy Goat, and blue for Big Billy Goat
- draw something else in three different sizes for the three goats

 Home Connection
Today we heard a story called *The Three Billy Goats Gruff*. Let me tell it to you. Listen for what each one says to the troll under the bridge and how he says it.

273

Name _____

THEME 9: Spring Is Here
Week Three *The Three Billy Goats Gruff*
Responding

Children
- draw something they would like to see on the big hill
- draw someone under the bridge
- draw someone on the bridge

Home Connection
Let me tell you about the pictures I drew. Then let's make up a story about my pictures and figure out a way to get to the hill besides over the bridge.

274

Name _____

1.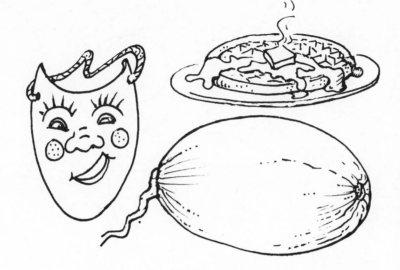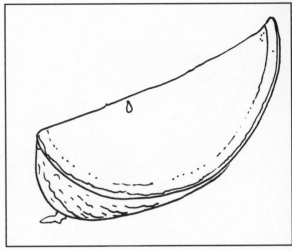

2.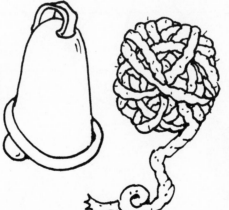

THEME 9: Spring Is Here
Week Three
Phonemic Awareness Review: /w/

Children
1. color the pictures whose names begin like *Willy Worm* and complete the watermelon picture
2. color the pictures whose names begin like *Yetta Yo-Yo* and complete the yak picture

Home Connection
Let's name all the things on the page that start like *Willy Worm* and *Yetta Yo-Yo*. Then we can find words in a book that start the same. You can read the words to me.

275

Name _____

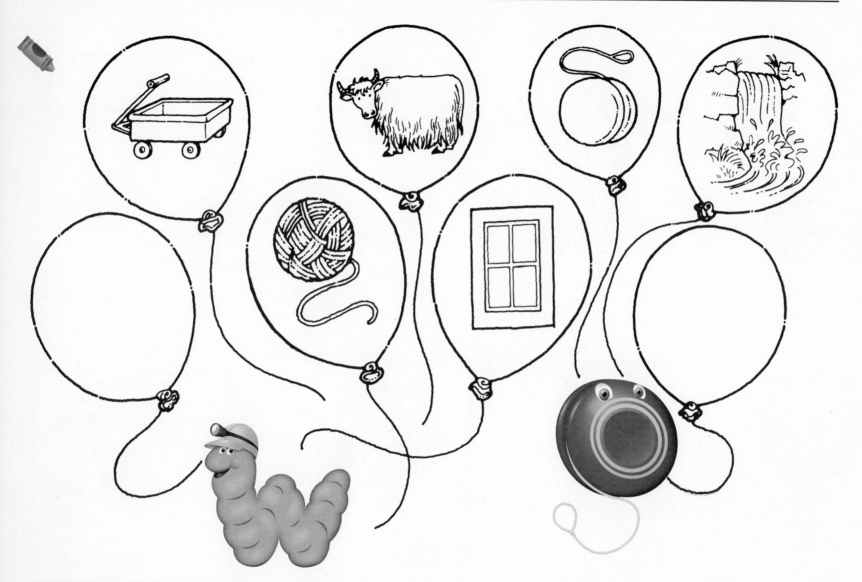

Children
- color blue Willy Worm's balloon and all the pictures that start like *Willy Worm*
- color yellow Yetta Yo-Yo's balloon and all the pictures that start like *Yetta Yo-Yo*

 Home Connection
Let's play this game: I'll say, "blue balloon" or "yellow balloon." Then you name something that starts like *Willy Worm* for blue or something that starts like *Yetta Yo-Yo* for yellow.

276

Name _____

Ww Yy

THEME 9: Spring Is Here
Week Three
Phonics Review: Initial Consonants *w, y*

Children
• name the letters at the top
• name the pictures *Willy Worm* and *Yetta Yo-Yo* think about
• color and write *w* or *y* next to the pictures whose names start with the sounds for those letters

 Home Connection
Next time we drive somewhere, let's look for things whose names start with the sounds for *w* or *y*.

277

Name _____

She   play

1. Can my cat _____ ?

2. _____ can play.

3. Can my big pig _____ ?

4. _____ can not play!

THEME 9: Spring Is Here
Week Three
High-Frequency Words Review: *play, she*

Children
- read the sentences and write *play* or *She* to complete what the people say
- color the cartoon

Home Connection
After I read this cartoon to you, I'll draw a new cartoon and make up some more sentences with *play* and *she*. You can write my sentences in speech balloons to go with my pictures.

278

Name _____

THEME 9: Spring Is Here
Week Three *Mrs. McNosh Hangs Up Her Wash*
Categorize and Classify

Children
- color things to wear yellow
- color things to eat red
- draw and color one more thing to wear and one more thing to eat that Mrs. McNosh could hang on her line

Home Connection
Can you figure out why I colored some of the things yellow and other things red? Let's name more kinds of things to wear and more kinds of things to eat.

279

y	w	h

	e	n

The pen is for the

_____

_____ .

	e	t

The big van is not here

_____

_____ .

	e	t

The big van is here

_____

_____

and it is _____ .

 THEME 9: Spring Is Here
Week Three
Phonics: -et, -en

Children
- write the letters to complete the words *hen*, *yet*, and *wet*
- write each word to finish the sentences

 Home Connection
We can cut out the letter squares, mix them up, and use them to spell *yet*, *wet*, and *hen*. Then we can find the matching picture for each word.

yet   ten   wet

  1.

_____
- - - - - - - - - - -

Is the fox _____?

☺ ☹

2.

_____
- - - - - - - - - - -

Is the pan hot _____?

☺ ☹

3.

_____
- - - - - - - - - - -

Can _____ men sit here?

☺ ☹

THEME 9: Spring Is Here
Week Three
Phonics: -et, -en

Children
- look at the pictures, read the questions, and write words to complete them
- mark the smile (yes) or the frown (no) to show their answer to the questions

 Home Connection
I can read these sentences to you! We can write the letters *y*, *e*, *t*, *n*, and *w* on separate scraps of paper and use them to build the words I wrote again.

Name _____

1.

"Here is my play kit,"

_____

_____ Nan.

2. _____

"I like the _____

kit," said Dan.

3. _____

"Jan said _____ can

get ten hats."

4.

"Jan can get the hats for

_____

_____ play," said Dan.

THEME 9: Spring Is Here
Week Three
High-Frequency Words Review: *play, she, said, the*

Children
• read the sentences and write *play, she, said,* or *the* to complete them
• color the pictures

Home Connection
Let me read you these sentences. Then let's make up other sentences with these words in them. Will you write down our sentences so I can find the words *play, she, said,* and *the*?

282

Name _____

1.

2.

3.

**THEME 10: A World of Animals
Week One Run Away!
Beginning, Middle, End**

Children
- think about what happened at the beginning and at the end of the story
- draw a picture in box 2 that shows something that happened in the story after Little Rabbit started running away and before all the animals went back to sleep again

 Home Connection
Let me tell you the story *Run Away!* I'll point to the pictures as I tell that part of the story.

283

Name _____

1.

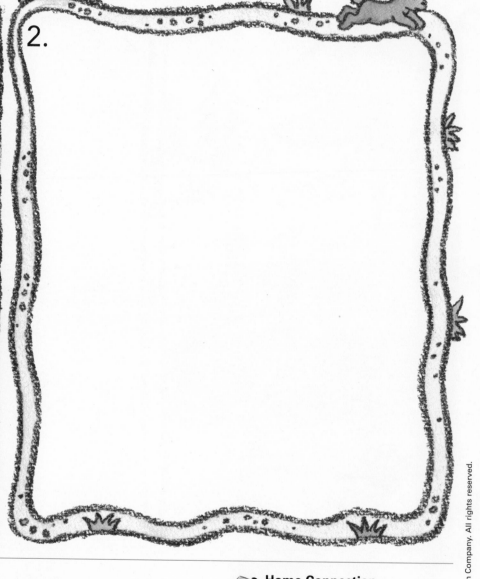

2.

THEME 10: A World of Animals
Week One Run Away!
Responding

Children

1. draw a picture to show what Little Rabbit thought was chasing him

2. think about something besides the wind in the tree branches that might have frightened rabbit and the other animals and draw a picture of your idea

 Home Connection
Today we heard a story called *Run Away!* I can tell you about it while you look at my pictures.

284

Name

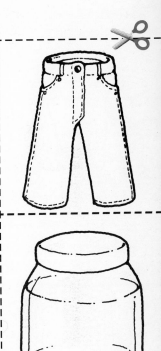

THEME 10: A World of Animals
Week One
Phonemic Awareness: /j/

Children
- color all the pictures on pages 285 and 286 that start like *Jumping Jill*
- cut and paste the pictures for that sound in the boxes on page 286
- draw something else that starts with that sound

 Home Connection
Let's name some things around the house that start like *Jumping Jill*.

285

THEME 10: A World of Animals
Week One
Phonemic Awareness: /j/

Name _____

1.

J j

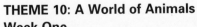

2.  j J j   J   j

THEME 10: A World of Animals
Week One
Phonics: Initial Consonant j

Children
1. draw lines from pictures whose names start with the sound for *j* to *Jj*
2. draw something else for that sound in the box with Jumping Jill

 Home Connection
Can you help me look through magazines for pictures of things whose names begin like *Jumping Jill?*

287

Name _____

are

1.

Dan and I _____ at

the . ☺ ☹

2.

Dan and I _____ hot.

☺ ☹

3.

Jan and Nat _____ at

the 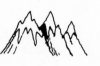 . ☺ ☹

4.

Jan and Nat _____ not
hot.

THEME 10: A World of Animals
Week One
High-Frequency Word *are*

Children
• read the sentences and write *are* to complete them
• mark the smile (yes) or the frown (no) to show whether the picture goes with the sentence
• draw a picture to go with sentence 4

Home Connection
I've learned to read the word *are* and I wrote it to finish the sentences in this short story. Let me read it to you.

Name _____

1 2 3

THEME 10: A World of Animals
Week One Splash!
Beginning, Middle, End; Responding

Children
- think about what happened in the story and color the picture of what happened at the beginning
- write *1*, *2*, and *3* below the pictures to show what happened at the beginning, in the middle and at the end of the story

 Home Connection
Today we heard a story called *Splash!* I'll tell it to you. I'll hold up one finger when I'm telling the beginning, two fingers when I'm telling the middle, and three fingers when I'm telling the end.

289

Name _____

  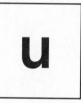 | u | g

See the cat and the

_____

_____?

 | u | g

_____

The big _____ can
go here.

 | u | g

_____

Here is my _____.

 THEME 10: A World of Animals
Week One
Phonics: *j, -ug*

Children
- write letters to complete the picture names
  (*rug, jug, mug*)
- write each word to complete the sentences
  that go with the pictures

 Home Connection
Let's think of some words that
end with the sounds at the end
of *rug, jug,* and *mug.* Then we
can make up some silly rhymes
with the words.

290

Name _____

 **u** **g**

Can she see the _____?

 **u** **g**

I can _____ it.

 **u** **g**

Can the _____ fit here?

THEME 10: A World of Animals
Week One
Phonics: -ug Words

Children
- add letters to -ug to build the words *bug*, *tug*, and *jug*
- write each word to complete the sentences that go with the pictures

 Home Connection
Let me read these sentences to you. Then maybe we can draw more pictures to go with the words *tug*, *bug*, and *jug*.

291

Are   play   she

1. _____

I can _____ the
hen.

2. _____

Jan said _____ can play
the cat.

3. _____

_____ Dan and Nan
here?

4. Dan can play the pig.
Nan can play the fox.

THEME 10: A World of Animals
Week One
High-Frequency Words Review: *are, play, she*

Children
- read the sentences and write *play, she,* and *Are* to complete them
- draw a picture to go with the sentences in 4

Home Connection
I've learned to read the words *are, play,* and *she.* Let me read this short story to you. Then we can make up an ending for it using the words I wrote.

Name _____

THEME 10: A World of Animals
Week Two *The Tale of the Three Little Pigs*
Compare and Contrast

Children
- compare the houses and color two things that are the same on all three
- find and circle something on the houses that is different on all three
- put a red mark on the house in the story that was the strongest

 Home Connection
Today we heard a story called *The Tale of the Three Little Pigs*. Do you know that story? Let me tell it to you. I'll try to use different voices for the pigs and for the wolf.

293

Name _____

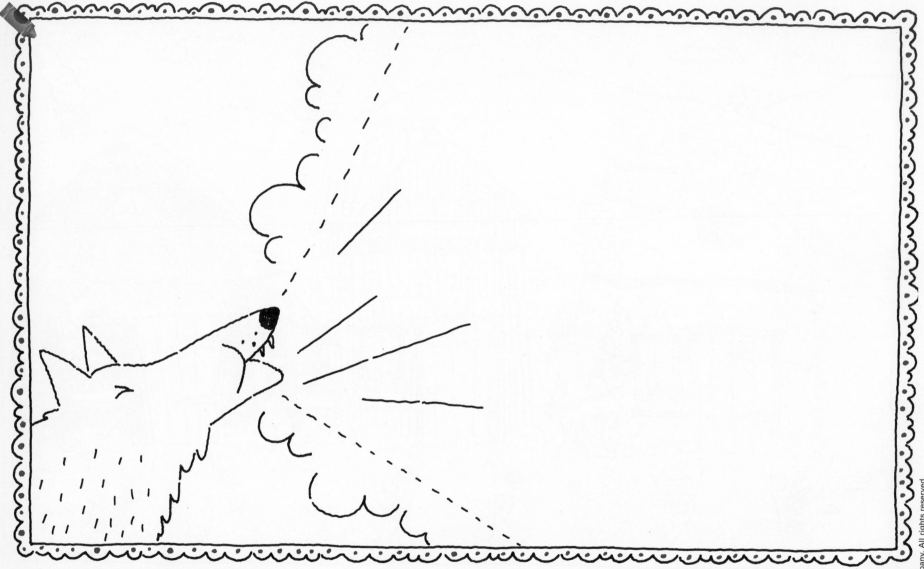

THEME 10: A World of Animals
Week Two *The Tale of the Three Little Pigs*
Responding

Children
- draw a picture of a house they would have built to protect themselves from the wolf or from a big, bad storm

 Home Connection
Let me tell you about the strong house I drew. Do you think it's strong enough to keep the wolf out? What do you think the wolf might say when he can't blow my house down?

1.

2.

3.

THEME 10: A World of Animals
Week Two
Phonemic Awareness Review: /l/, /b/, /c/

Children

1. color the pictures whose names start like *Larry Lion* and complete the leopard picture
2. color the pictures whose names start like *Benny Bear* and complete the boat picture
3. color the pictures whose names start like *Callie Cat* and complete the cake picture

Home Connection
Let me name the pictures I colored. Then you can help me think of other things whose names start like *Larry Lion*, *Benny Bear*, and *Callie Cat*.

295

Name _____

THEME 10: A World of Animals
Week Two
Phonemic Awareness Review: /l/, /b/, /c/

Children
- color red Larry Lion's balloon and the pictures whose names start like *Larry Lion*
- color blue Benny Bear's balloon and the pictures whose names start like *Benny Bear*
- color yellow Callie Cat's balloon and the pictures whose names start like *Callie Cat*

 Home Connection
I'll name the picture on each balloon, and you can name the matching Alphafriend.

Name _____

Ll Bb Cc

THEME 10: A World of Animals
Week Two
Phonics Review: Initial Consonants _l, b, c_

Children
- color all the pictures
- write _l_ beside pictures whose names start like _Larry Lion_, _b_ beside pictures whose names start like _Benny Bear_, and _c_ beside pictures whose names start like _Callie Cat_

 Home Connection
I'll tell you which pictures start with the sounds for _l_, for _b_, and for _c_. Next time we go somewhere, let's look for other things that start with these sounds.

Name _____

he

_____

Dan said _____ can fit.

_____

Nat said _____ can not fit.

Children
• read the sentences and write *he* to complete them
• color the pictures

Home Connection
Let me read these sentences to you. Then we can make up more sentences with *he* and you can help me write them.

Name _____

1.

2.

THEME 10: A World of Animals
Week Two *Feathers for Lunch*
Compare and Contrast, Responding

Children
- think about how cats and birds are different
- color red the things the cat might like and yellow the things the bird might like
- draw something both cats and birds might like

 Home Connection
Next time we take a walk, we can compare the animals we see. We can compare their sizes, their colors, their markings, the sounds they make, and what they are doing.

299

Name _____

cut   hut   but

Can you _____ a pan?

Nan can go, _____ I can not.

She ran to a _____ .

 THEME 10: A World of Animals
Week Two
Phonics: b, c, -ut

Children
• read the questions and write *cut*, *but*, and *hut* to complete them
• mark the smile (yes) or the frown (no) to show their answers to the sentences

Home Connection
Let's write *cut*, *but*, and *hut* on separate scraps of paper. Then we can turn the words face down and take turns picking one and making up a sentence with that word.

300

Name _____

b	→	ut	_____
c	→	ut	_____
n	→	ut	_____

I like the box _____ not the hat.

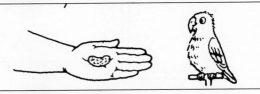

Is the _____ for my pet?

"I can _____ it," said Nan.

THEME 10: A World of Animals
Week Two
Phonics: -ut Words

Children
- add letters to -ut to build the words *but*, *cut*, and *nut*
- write each word to complete the sentences that go with the pictures

 Home Connection
Let me read these sentences to you. Then maybe we can draw more pictures to go with the words *but*, *cut*, and *nut*.

301

Name _____

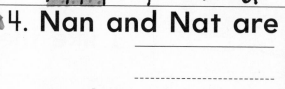

he   Are   she   play

1. _____

Is _____ a cat?

2. _____

Is _____ a fox?

3. _____

_____ Nan and Nat

here?

4. Nan and Nat are

_____

at the _____.

THEME 10: A World of Animals
Week Two
High-Frequency Words Review: *he, are,*
she, play

Children
• read the sentences and write *he, she, are,* and
  play to complete them
• draw a picture for sentence 4

 Home Connection
Let me read these sentences to
you. Then let's make up a new
story about Nat and Nan who
are in the play instead of just
watching it.

Name _____

THEME 10: A World of Animals
Week Three _Henny Penny_
Plot

Children
- think about what happens in the story and draw a line through the two pictures in the story map that show something that did not happen
- draw a picture that shows what Foxy Loxy probably hoped would happen in the end

 Home Connection
I can use the story map to help me tell you about the problem the animals had in the story _Henny Penny_. Then I'll tell you how they solved their problem.

303

THEME 10: A World of Animals
Week Three *Henny Penny*
Responding

Children
- think about and draw what Foxy Loxy did for his dinner after Henny Penny and her friends got away

Home Connection
Let me tell you about my pictures.

Name _____

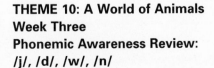

THEME 10: A World of Animals
Week Three
Phonemic Awareness Review:
/j/, /d/, /w/, /n/

Children
- color the pictures on pages 305 and 306 whose names start like *Jumping Jill, Dudley Duck, Willy Worm,* or *Nyle Noodle*
- cut and paste pictures whose names start like these sounds in the boxes beside their matching Alphafriends on page 306

🏠 **Home Connection**
Let's look in our kitchen cabinets to find things whose names begin like *Jumping Jill, Dudley Duck, Willy Worm,* or *Nyle Noodle.*

305

Name _____

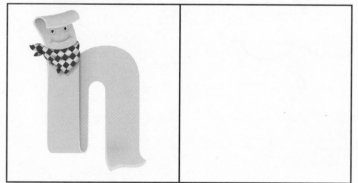

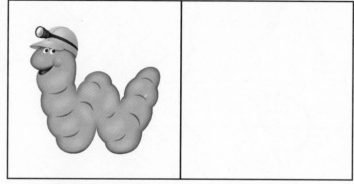

Name _____

1. | **Jj Dd Ww Nn** |

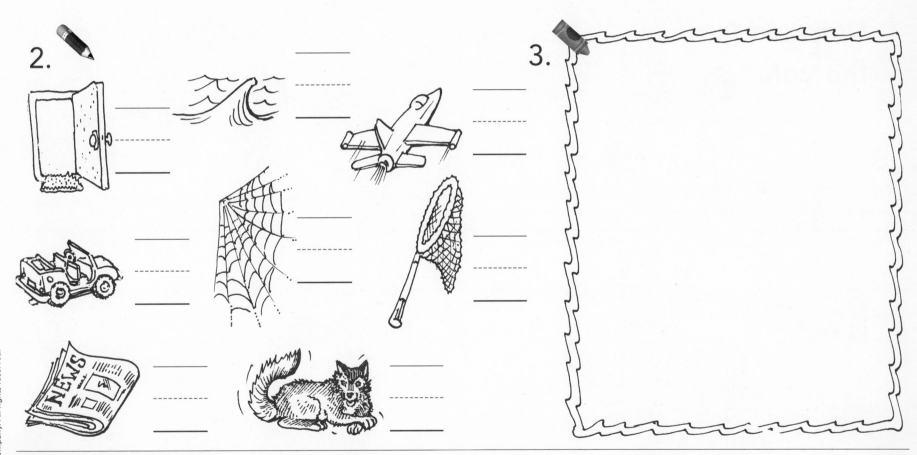

2.

3.

THEME 10: A World of Animals
Week Three
Phonics Review: Initial Consonants _j, d, w, n_

Children

1. name the letters at the top
2. write _j, d, w,_ or _n_ beside the picture whose name begins with the sound for that letter
3. circle a letter at the top and draw two more things that start with the sound for that letter

 Home Connection
Let's name the pictures on the page and tell the letter each begins with. You can do the things that begin with the sound for _d_ and for _w_ and I'll do the ones for _n_ and for _j._

307

Name _____

He   Are   are

1. _____

Nan and Nat _____ at

the van.

2. _____

_____ Dan and Pat

here?

3. _____

_____ is here but she

is not.

4. _____

Pat and Cat _____ at

the .

THEME 10: A World of Animals
Week Three
High-Frequency Words Review: _are, he_

308

Children
• read the sentences and write _he_ and _are_ to complete them
• draw a picture for sentence 4

Home Connection
Let me read these sentences to you. Then let's make up a new story about Nat and Nan who are riding in a van.

Name _____

1.

2.

3.

THEME 10: A World of Animals
Week Three _Feathers for Lunch_
Plot, Responding

Children
- color the pictures in the row that shows what happened in _Feathers for Lunch_
- think of a story they could tell for each of the other rows of pictures

 Home Connection
Let me tell you a story for each row of pictures. The first row is about a story I heard called _Feathers for Lunch_. Then maybe you can tell me a different story for each row of pictures.

309

Name _____

  [ ] **u** **g** _____

I _____ and got a box.

   [ ] **u** **g** _____

The _____ is for Dan.

  [ ] **u** **t** _____

I have a _____ for the .

THEME 10: A World of Animals
Week Three
Phonics: *j, d, n, -ug, -ut*

Children
- write the letters to complete the picture names (*dug, jug,* and *nut*)
- write the words *dug, jug,* and *nut* to complete the sentences

Home Connection
Ask me to read these sentences to you. Then we can cut out the letter squares, mix them up, and use them to make *jug, dug* and *nut* again.

310

rug   nut   jug

_____

Is the _____ for the man?

_____

Is the _____ for Dan?

_____

Is the _____ for the cat?

THEME 10: A World of Animals
Week Three
Phonics: -ug, -ut Words

Children
- read the questions and write words to complete them
- mark the smile (yes) or the frown (no) to show whether the pictures answer the questions

Home Connection
Let's make up some more questions like the ones on this page. Can you think of any other words that end like *jug* or *nut* that we could use in our questions?

311

Name _____

| are | He | play | she |

1. Is Nan here and can

_____

_____ play?

2. ---------------

She can _____ but

Nat can not.

3. _____

_____ is at the 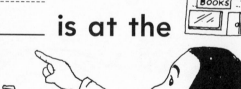 .

4. ---------------

Nan and Jan _____

here to play.

THEME 10: A World of Animals
Week Three
High-Frequency Words Review:
are, he, play, she

Children
- read the sentences and write *she, play, he,* and *are* to complete them
- draw a picture to go with sentence 4

Home Connection
Let me read these sentences to you. Then let's make up some more sentences for this short story. You can write the sentence down so I can look for these words in them.

313

Name _____